HOW TO BECOME A
SOCIAL
INFLUENCER

Build a Brand
Work for Yourself
Become Incredibly Successful

Table of Contents

Introduction

Part 1: Who Are You and What Will You Do?

Part 2: Getting Started as a Social Influencer

Part 3: Building Your Brand

Part 4: Business Lessons 101

How to Become a Social Influencer

A Dream or a Plan?

It seems that everyone now wants to become a social influencer and wield tremendous power that can manifest virtually endless financial success. The problem is that most people who know how to actually gain influence do not want to share their real secrets of success and everyone else is basically clueless about how to start, how to grow and how to dominate in a highly competitive industry.

There has never been a more exciting time on the internet! People from all over the world have the chance to build amazing businesses based on what they LOVE to do and WHO they are. This type of influencer business does not require a monetary investment, but does require lots of hard work. If you think that being an influencer is easy, then you are in for a real shock!

People associate influencers as living rockstar lifestyles and for sure, the most successful of them truly do. However, just like starting a band, you don't make it to Billboard's Top 10 in a week. You have to apply yourself, improve your skills, make connections, get noticed, gain fans and continuously struggle upstream against some very tough competition.

I have read so many articles on becoming an influencer and most of them focus on how to capitalize on your success. However, few of these resources actually walk you through the process on how to begin building your brand and how NOT to potentially waste years' of time going about things the wrong way. This is why I wanted to write this concise ebook. My goal is to help you begin from day 1 of your new business venture and elevate you to a level where your own hard-earned organic knowledge will take you the rest of the way to super stardom. Are you ready to start? Let's get going together and start building!

What is a Social Influencer?

Influencers are people who do just what their name implies: They exert influence on people who follow them (followers) and value their opinion and work. Social influencers establish themselves as authorities in a specific genre called a niche and then build up a base of followers. Influencers will work hard to connect with their audience and earn loyal support through their knowledge, creativity, authority and personality. The more followers an influencer can attain, and the more engaged these followers are, the more valuable the influencer becomes. A popular influencer can literally make or break brands simply by offering their opinion. This is immense power and this type of influence can lead to tremendous profitability, as well.

Influencers exist in every possible genre. Influencers can be very general, such as a fashion influencer, travel influencer or even lifestyle influencer, or highly specific, such as a DIY pickle-making influencer! There is no genre too large or too small to work in. However, it is best to define yourself in a highly specific niche in order to minimize competition and establish a real definable identity and knowledge base to share with your audience. I always recommend entering a niche where you already have passion and knowledge. The passion will keep you motivated and the knowledge will help your new career to get off in a positive direction for success. You should not enter a niche simply because you feel that it is popular or presents a good opportunity right now. When it comes to finding your niche, it is best to decide with your head and heart... (knowledge and passion!)

Influencers can discuss, review, promote or criticize anything they want. They can discuss, review, promote or criticize social, political or environmental causes. They can discuss, review, promote or criticize products or services that they might offer or those offered by other companies or individuals. They can become brand ambassadors for firms that share a common point of view (POV) and interests. Influencers can also simply work to propagate an industry in general, showing allegiance to no specific brand, but furthering the interests of their entire subject focus as a whole. This is particularly true for influencers who have been doing this job for a very long time and have gained respect from friends, followers and even adversaries alike!

Who can be an influencer? In essence, anyone can! You do not need to be a celebrity or a household name. A literal army of people make excellent livings being influencers, even though YOU and MOST PEOPLE might have no idea who they are or what they do. They work in niches that are not mainstream and they will never become famous in the general population. However, in their specific areas of expertise, they are the GO-TO names for reliable information and opinions that might sway thousands, millions or more when it comes to economic transactions.

In essence, influencers are all around you. They are celebrities and they are your neighbors next door. Anyone who has knowledge and provides an opinion on anything can be influential. The thing that separates a professional influencer from just a "normal person" is their deep investment in building a career based on their ability to influence, rather than simply being content to follow others. Professional influencers are the leaders of today and have become a multibillion dollar industry unto themselves.

Do you want to become a professional influencer? The idea holds great appeal for many people. You can work in any industry you choose. You can love your work. You can work anywhere in the world in many cases. You can get paid BIG to do what you enjoy most. These are all really strong selling points to become a professional social influencer. However, I must tell you right from the beginning that this is a very difficult job to do… If you believe that you can just say whatever you want on a website or social platform and get paid, then you are in for a rude awakening!

You will have to work hard for a very long time against really tough competition. You will have to develop skills that you might not currently possess. You will have to be consistent and disciplined, working every day to improve yourself and your brand. There is no guarantee that you will make it as an influencer. But, if you try hard, you can do it! You do not have to be particularly smart, beautiful, creative, talented or any other special thing. You just have to be willing to do what I mention above.

The number one factor that separates successful influencers from everyone else is their ability to work hard consistently over long timelines. If you can do this, then you have every opportunity to succeed and create a life you can only dream of right now! If you want a quick fix for a unsatisfying life, then try playing the lottery. You have a better chance of winning than you will of transforming yourself into a successful and well paid influencer overnight!

However, if you can be patient, determined, motivated, humble, hungry and driven by the right ideals, then there is absolutely no reason why YOU can not do this business successfully. You CAN become an influencer and take your success to incredible heights. Are you ready to get started? Make a commitment to yourself right now before going any further...
Let's say these things together:

- "I want to be my own boss."

- "I choose to invest in myself and create my own brand."

- "I will not quit."

- "I am not afraid to work hard every day."

- "I will succeed."

You can say these things to yourself every day in fact. It is great to reaffirm your commitment as often as possible. Don't simply say the words. Feel the meaning inside your heart and engrave the commitment into your soul. Ready? Let's move forward!

Why Do I Want to Become an Influencer?

People each have different individual paths up the mountain of success, with many reasons for climbing. At the base of this mountain, many people are standing around looking upwards. Most of these people are gawking idly. Some are thinking about climbing. Many people are commenting about others who just started to ascend. "They will never make it" can be heard throughout the crowd of onlookers. Others start on the journey, but quickly realize that the path is steep and somewhat difficult. They soon give up and go back down. These individuals account for 99% of all people who set out to become influencers. Only 1% will continue to climb and work hard to make tangible gains. Some gains will be large, but most will be small...literally one tiny step at a time up the steep slope.

Towards the top, people who have traversed many separate paths from many different places around the base of the mountain can now see each other clearly. The amount of real estate on the mountain gets smaller as climbers get higher. There is only room for so many as you ascend. The top of the mountain awaits, but only the very best will make it to the pinnacle. The competition at this point isn't easier. It is exponentially more challenging. Many, many people attempt to scale Mount Everest, but how many successfully summit? Incredibly few... This is the reality of top level influencers, as well!

You will have to summon all of your skills, perseverance and determination in order to make those last few steps to actually become a top tier influencer... in order to reach the pinnacle of the mountain. Can you do it? That might just depend on why you want to become an influencer in the first place...

People have all types of reasons for wanting to become a social influencer. These motivations will weigh heavily on a person's ability to actually succeed in their endeavor, so finding the right motivation is crucial! Let's explore some common motivations for wanting to become an influencer:

- Make money

- Become a celebrity

- Build a sustainable business

- Work for oneself

- Propagate specific knowledge

- Support an industry or ideology

- Take advantage of social connections or position

- Desire to help people

- Desire to be a critic

If you want to become an influencer just to be famous or make money, your chances of success are very low. If you have a deeper motivation to become an influencer, like a real love for your niche or a desire to do good things for people or your industry, then you have a much better chance of staying the course and finding eventual success.

As noted previously, there are many paths up the mountain of success. However, all paths lead to the summit and the great rewards which await there. However, the even more universal truth is that every path is individual and difficult. There is no easy way up this mountain and no way to insure you can stay at the peak once you arrive.

You might fall from the summit due to your own mistakes. You might be pushed off by a competitor. You might simply be left standing alone on the mountain while your audience is now watching what is going on at a completely different mountain altogether! Remember, some influencers simply become irrelevant if their playing field disappears (remember Myspace?), even without any catastrophic occurrence ruining their careers.

Will I Be Able to Become an Influencer?

Yes. Anyone can become an influencer. There are no definitive qualifications, attributes or criteria necessary. That being said, there are many things which will help you to succeed and many things that will pose serious impediments to your success. Therefore, in the interest of self-evaluation, let's spend a bit of time trying to figure out how likely it is you will succeed as a social influencer and what changes you can make to assist you in accomplishing your dreams.

Optimal Attributes and Conditions for Influencer Success

Let's first look at some of the personal attributes and life conditions that are very valuable for people to have when pursuing an influencer career:

- Intelligence never hurts in any endeavor. Being smart and doing smart will make everything better for you in your new career. Always think before you act.

- Creativity is necessary. All influencers must be creative to some extent. Even those who simply critique and evaluate the work of others must still share their opinions creatively or no one will listen.

- Patience is more than a virtue; it's a necessity! Being successful will take time. It might take a very long time. You must keep you eye on your goals and work steadily towards them each day until you succeed.

- You MUST be capable of working hard. This is NOT an easy job. You should be a hustler and capable of being responsible in everything you do.

- You MUST be capable of working consistently. Make and keep a schedule for work-related tasks. Stick to this schedule NO MATTER WHAT.

- You must have a solid and doable business plan or at least evolve one as you grow. Understand how to set goals, strategize to reach these goals and re-evaluate your objectives when problems occur.

- You should have lots of time to work on your new business. Working a full time job or being in school can greatly limit your productivity. Ideally, you will be able to focus being an influencer as a full-time gig. If not, you will have to be very dedicated and be prepared to prioritize what you MUST do over what you WANT to do in your spare time!

- If you have some money to support yourself, it will take pressure off, especially when you first get started. This is why many influencers have previous work experience in online businesses, since they are able to build a passive, or at least semi-passive income, that will sustain them as they work on a new venture. I highly recommend this path, as I am one who has followed it myself. I have earned every dollar I have online since 2006 and have done it honestly, ethically and even helpfully to our planet and the people on it. I am proud of my work, which brings its own satisfaction... financial gains aside!

Detrimental Attributes and Conditions to Influencer Success

The following attributes and life conditions will not make being a successful influencer impossible, but will present distinct challenges for you in your new chosen career path. Do everything you can to rectify these issues BEFORE investing yourself in your new influencer business! If not, work on correcting them as you move forward in your new career...

- If you are only focused on the end game of being a successful influencer (being rich, party-lifestyle), it is highly unlikely that you will ever attain success. Be realistic. You will have to work hard in order to succeed. No work, no success...

- You might not have natural gifts of talent, creativity or intelligence as detailed above. However, you can still acquire these attributes. Start today! Work on enriching yourself in order to become better at that you do. The more capable you become in all things, the better an influencer you will be. Invest in you!

- If you are very busy, it will be difficult to find time to work on everything you will need to do to become a really successful influencer. Therefore, try to free up time and set this time aside to work exclusively on your new venture.

- Likewise, set aside some money and re-evaluate your expenses and lifestyle unless you are rich to begin with. If you can spend less and need less money, then you can afford to spend more time working on your new business and less time earning at a "day job" just to pay your bills. This sacrifice takes a denial of ego and of worldly wants now, with the tradeoff of potentially building a very lucrative business in the future. There is risk involved here and you must accept it. If you are obsessed with security in life, then pursuing an influencer career is not your best bet!

Take some time to really consider these points and how they apply to you. If you fit the type of person who is likely to succeed, then do not even pause. Just keep reading and let's get to work! If not, take some time to evaluate what changes you can make to yourself and your life in order to facilitate success as a social influencer before leaping head first into the profession.

If you have changed your mind and realize that you are probably not up to the task (which is fine!), then you might just decide to forget about becoming an influencer and pursue some other path. You can still do many businesses which will allow you to reach similar goals in life, especially online. If this is your decision, please continue on your destined path in life and find success in whatever you choose to do! Better to know and move forward positively then to waste time and effort on a lost cause...

I am Ready to Start Earning!

No, you're probably not. Not by a long shot... but at least you want to go ahead and pursue your dream of becoming an influencer. That a great sign! Do you know how many people talk about doing this job, but actually never do anything about it? Just taking the fundamental steps forward already puts you in a category of people who have true potential to succeed.

My very first practical piece of advice on your quest is to forget all about money. Don't make it a priority. Don't set it as one of your major goals. Not yet at least... If you are focused on the endgame of your influencer success, then you will never be able to focus on all the component things that you must be in order to achieve that success. Just FORGET MONEY for now.

Being an influencer is a business proposition. However, like many other internet-based businesses, you do not have to invest much real world financial capital in the endeavor upfront. You will have to invest some money for things like web hosting, file storage, subcontractor services and promotions. However, the major investments you will absolutely have to make are time and effort. You will have to invest heavily in sweat equity in order to succeed.

Work hard. Work consistently. Work smart. Work more than your competitors. This is the way to make it as an influencer now. Several years ago, it was much easier to reach the upper echelon of influencer success. Now, it is exponentially more difficult. You have to really apply yourself in order to stand out. Unless you have tons of money to invest, then working super diligently is the only path to take to the top of the success mountain.

I will talk to you much more about money as this book progresses, but for now, I want to be absolutely clear with you that it is extremely unlikely (virtually impossible) that you will make money quickly as an influencer. It is much more likely that you will have to work for several years before you make any real money and even that is not a given. You will have to earn the opportunity through your blood, sweat and tears and trust me, you will invest all three!

Some people are really focused on economics and would be much better off working a traditional job or starting a traditional business for sure, since the financial opportunities are more certain and usually, more lucrative. Therefore be warned, if money is your priority, being an influencer is NOT the best path to fulfilling your primary goal of financial independence.

However, being an influencer comes with many other benefits, such as independence, the ability to work from anywhere and the ability to really build an amazing brand empire over time, with virtually no monetary investment. Therefore, give your future some real thought before you decide on going any further...

Are you ready? Ok, you see the benefits of an influencer career and are determined to go ahead! Awesome! Let's move forward into the next part of the journey. Let's actually begin to formulate your business plan and blueprint your road to success! Now is where the real work begins. Get ready to embark. There is no time like right now to get going...

Part 1:
Who Are You and What Will You Do?

Ok, let's get down to business... It is time to start with action steps and stop just conceptualizing. If you are going to succeed, you MUST start somewhere, so let's commence at the very beginning and get you off in the right direction towards success. Baby steps will lead to grand accomplishments later on...

As you move forward with your business plan, take notes. Take LOTS of notes! You can do this however you choose, Just do not forget that a written account of your business plan will be invaluable now and will help you to succeed as you move forward. Don't rush! Planning will set the stage for your success or failure, so do it right.

Brainstorm Your Niche

What is a niche? Your niche? A niche is the focus of your influence. It can be anything at all or several things, in fact. Your niche can be a hobby, interest, subject, person, place, activity, event... anything at all. You can combine complementary niches to potentially become a super influencer with a vast reach into people's lives. You can substitute the word topic, subject, genre, focus, specialty or other any synonym you choose. However, understand that niche is the industry standard word, so use it and get acclimated to it! Let's look closer at niches...

Hobby niches can be anything from model airplanes to musical instruments. You might broaden your horizon to cover art in general or you might focus on finger-painting using charcoals only. You might want to talk about beauty or fashion or a specific aspect of these popular niches.

You might be interested in science or a specific cause. Maybe you are an environmentalist or a person who wants to work for women's rights. Do you love animals? Maybe they will become the focus of your influencer work.

Do you live somewhere special, or even somewhere very ordinary, and want to make that place your focus? Are you a New Yorker? Maybe you're living on a family farm in a rural area and want to talk about farm life. Travel is a very popular niche and leaves many possibilities to cover, from specific regions or destinations to specific budgets or ways of travel. You might even cover the logistics of travel, such as cruises or flights.

You might be a sports enthusiast. Maybe you cycle or climb. You may be one of the growing number of e-sports athletes who really excel at video games. Do you love camping or hiking? Those niches are easily combined with others to form a great sector to work in.

Food is a great focus. Everyone has to eat, right? Street food, gourmet food, fast food, alcoholic beverages... All of these topics are ideal influencer focuses.

Maybe you want to promote a specific event or set of events that recur every year, such as competitions, dog shows, beauty pageants, races. All of these niches can be great. Just make sure they are not one-off events or your career will end soon after the event finishes! Lol...

You can do lifestyle influence, as well. Maybe you want to promote a sustainable eco-friendly lifestyle or a healthy lifestyle. In these sectors, you might combine all the aspects of life that contribute to fulfill your niche objective.

Photography is a great niche, as is video production. Tutorials on anything are easily promoted and extremely monetizable. If you are really good at doing something, then definitely consider it as a part of your niche, if not the primary focus!

Here are some lesser considered examples of interesting niches: Anime, cosplay, comics, cars, all types of activism, makeup, beauty, entertainment and button collecting!

I could literally talk about niches for pages here and would barely scratch the surface. However, there is no need to list them all or even more than I already have. I only include these examples to get your creative juices flowing. You need to do what you WANT to do and LOVE to do. This is the most important thing!

Anything can be a niche!

Is My Niche Too Broad or Too Narrow?

I don't want you to worry too much about your long-term goals from day one. However, you do want to keep in mind the possibility for growth, competition and authority before you start working. Therefore, really think hard about which is the right niche for you to focus upon. You can fine tune this idea as you go and make subtle changes over time that will be capable of narrowing your niche or expanding it, if you choose.

However, you want to make absolutely sure that the niche will truly work for you before you begin to work on it... If not, then all your effort will be in vain and will result in taking the wind right out of your sails. Remember: Plan first, then actually do the work. Look for potential problems in a niche before committing to it!

It is really difficult to be in a niche which is too broad in the long-run. Many super successful influencers cover "lifestyle" including food, fashion, travel, activities and health. These are all huge topics unto themselves, but are all also highly complementary to one another. For a successful influencer, they can talk in less detail about each compartmentalized aspect of their niche and more about how to blend all their interests to formulate an idyllic lifestyle that anyone would like to emulate.

Keep in mind that few influencers will ever find real success going this very broad route from day one. Instead, most will focus on a more specific aspect of their larger lifestyle niche to gain momentum and minimize competition. As they grow and their influence grows with them, then they will slowly expand their authority by integrating new avenues of expression that are related and complementary. This is the best way to expand a niche or grow into a larger and more profitable niche to develop more influence.

Therefore, it is best to focus your niche somewhat narrowly to get started and add-in small bits of something different as you develop. Basically, work to become the big fish in the really small pond before leaping into a lake and finally, the ocean... You will have a much better chance of making it to the top of the success mountain going this route.

You might also quickly find that your niche is too broad and causes you to lose authority by diluting your coverage of specific and in-demand aspects of subniches. You might set out to be a fashion influencer, but soon realize that you are getting nowhere. You best work tends to be in men's formalwear, so you go back to basics and focus on that. You soon become known as an authority in this subniche topic and then interested people are now finding and following you. Don't be afraid to narrow your focus either as you move forward. You can always expand later as your influence expands also. It will certainly be easier to reach the very top of your niche if it is smaller and less competitive.

Your results will speaks volumes about the direction you should be headed. If you are growing and achieving where you are, there is no need to change anything as long as you are happy doing what you are doing now. Keep going and keep growing! If you need to broaden or narrow your niche, you will know soon enough, based on your results and how your followers interact with you.

A final piece of very important advice in this regard is as follows: If you have really in-depth knowledge and can honestly call yourself an expert in a particular niche, then go with it. The niche will be an organic fit. Focus on it and become the go-to person for that thing, no matter now narrow it may be. However, find complementary topics that might relate to your focus if the niche is restrictive and then slowly integrate these closely-related subjects into your influencer work also. This will give you plenty of opportunity to grow, while still maintaining your authority in your primary subject matter,

On the other hand, if you are interested in many things and consider yourself a renaissance person or a jack-of-all-trades, consider challenging yourself with a broader niche from day one. Showcase how balanced you are and why your way of combining knowledge makes your POV different, even if you lack complete dominance of expertise in each focus you cover. Be the true definition of a well-rounded person and make others want to follow you for ALL the things you do, rather than just a specific single thing. This approach can work also. Just know that this is a much, much more difficult path and relies much more heavily on you developing certain marketable skills or being naturally gifted with some special attribute, such as beauty, talent or charisma.

Take time to write down all your thoughts about possible niches so that you don't forget any good ideas as you are brainstorming. Think about working right now, as well as the future big picture when doing this work!

Ok, get to work. I want to see you spend some time and really write down as many ideas as come into your head. Don't leave anything off your list. Write down all your possibilities. Think about your life, your experience, your passions and all the things that make you YOU. Don't worry about what is in fashion or trendy right now. You should define you niche based on personal expertise and interest. Never let public opinion create your niche for you!

Once you have ideas on paper, take time to look at each idea and cross some off as you realize that they are not the best fit for you. In the end, you should be left with an obvious choice of niche or maybe 2 or 3 choices which will all work. Keep these options as your working niche(s) and let's move ahead to the next step. You need to know how to represent yourself to others. This is called your brand.

Brainstorm Your Brand

Once you have a good idea of what your niche will be, then you need to start coming up with ideas for your brand. Branding is a very important concept to any influencer to fully understand. If you are to become successful, you need to be more than just a person. You must become a recognized and respected business entity. This entity is your brand identify.

Branding is a very complex topic and the subject of many books unto itself. However, I will provide some guidance for you to consider and at least give you some branding strategies to choose from...

My very first piece of advice when it comes to branding is DON'T RUSH! Take your time, get outside opinions on the brand name, POV and image and then do lots of research to be absolutely sure that the branding you embrace will not have any liabilities associated with it. How do you go about doing all this? Ok, let's start with the basics:

How do you want to represent yourself? Do you want to use your real name? Maybe you want to use an alias instead. Do you want to create a brand name to represent your work; basically a company name? Write down some ideas and allow some room to take notes on each.

Then, think creatively. What can you do to improve on the brand names that you like? You can add things to a name or alias to make them more memorable. You can also take things away from a name to simplify it or make it easier to remember.

Your brand should be catchy. It should be memorable. A brand is much more than a name. It is a vision that represents who you are and what you will be doing. If an identifier of the niche of your influence appears in the name, it might be beneficial, but it is not necessary by any means. For example, if you will be focused on the ocean, you might want to include the words "ocean" or "sea" in your brand name. Be creative. Be clever!

Branding goes far beyond the name. You must envision what it is that your brand will stand for:

- What is important to you?

- What is your mission?

- What value will your brand provide for people?

- What kind of influence do you seek to have and how will you utilize this influence?

These are all concepts to start thinking about during the branding phase. They do not have to be set in stone, but the basic outline of your brand should begin to crystallize as you brainstorm names.

Ok, so now you have some ideas. Don't do anything yet! Now it is time to look at whether anyone is using these names already. You definitely DO NOT want to use a name that is already in existence and associated with another brand. This can create huge liabilities when it comes to registering your brand on social networks and on the web, as well as potentially exposing yourself to intellectual property rights violations. Therefore, check your favorite social networks and try the brand name as a URL.

For example, if you like "Jammy Journey" for a name, type in JammyJourney.com and see what comes up. If there is nothing there, try Jammy-Journey.com, JammyJourney.net and JammyJourney.Org to see if this brand already exists. Do a Google search using just the brand name and look through the first page of results. What does a search of Jammy Journey provide on Google? If the brand already exists in ANY form, do not consider it. Scratch it off your list immediately. (Yes, many people register brands that are similar in spelling to known brands. Example – Starrbucks. This is an underhanded strategy that will NEVER attract quality followers. It might also set you up for some serious civil liabilities. DO NOT do this!)

Now repeat this search on your favorite social media platforms. Definitely include YouTube, Facebook, Twitter and Instagram. If this name already is in use, then you will certainly know it by now and will have to abandon it in favor of another idea. If it is clear and available, then you are good to go with the brand. Check to see if you can register a Gmail account under this brand name or if it is already taken. However, don't move ahead to registering anything yet...

Instead, take a bit of time to consider the brand. Think about how it will look in print and how universally appealing it might be. Does the brand name and image speak to people? Is it easy to spell and remember? Will people like it? Ask some close friends for their opinions, without showing your partiality to a specific name. Ask them to consider 3 or 4 of the names you have come up with and then use their feedback to guide your final decision. Once you have done your due diligence and really taken your time to formulate a strong brand name and identity, then it is time to register your brand. This will be your first giant leap forward towards success as a social influencer!

Helpful Tip: Do NOT be one of those people who post your brainstorming ideas on a public forum asking for opinions, unless of course you want them to be stolen right from under your nose. Keep your brand name and concept quiet; just between you and trusted friends or family, until everything is officially registered.

Register Your Brand

Now go to all the social networks that you are currently using and register your brand name. YOU MUST BE UNIFORM! Make absolutely sure to use the exact same name, same spelling, etc in every platform! There can be NO EXCEPTIONS to this rule! Even if you have no intention on using a specific social platform, be absolutely sure to register your name there or someone else will and this can cause HUGE problems for you later on.

Cover yourself on Facebook, Instagram, Twitter and any secondary social media platform you intend on using or any you fear someone may try to use with your brand identity.

For YouTube, there is an immediate problem apparent... You can not name your actual channel until you have at least 100 subscribers. You can use your name as the user name, but you will have to work hard (beg your friends and family —whatever it takes) to get those first 100 subscribers quickly so that you can secure your brand name on YouTube as soon as possible. If you already have an existing personal channel with subscribers, then you might be able to convert it to business use and rename it right away. If you are not using YouTube, then this becomes a much less important priority, but should still be attended to as a placeholder precaution for the future should you embrace using a video channel later on in your influencer career.

Simultaneously, register your domain name, which should also be your brand. The closer you can get it to the actual brand name the better! Try not to use hyphens or dashes in the name, unless of course, they are also part of your actual brand name! You will want to have a .com address. Let me repeat this...
YOU WANT .COM OK?

If you want to be safe, you can also register other permutations, like .net, .org, .tv, or some other specific TLD if you like, to reduce the chances of someone stealing your name or impersonating you. Domains are becoming more expensive than in the past, so do not go too crazy trying to protect yourself by registering every possible permutation. It will still not really protect you and will cost too much money over time!

Get a Gmail account with your brand name. Once again, do not deviate from the brand name or spelling in any way if at all possible. Due to the demand for Gmail accounts, some brands run into their first snag here, since the address might be taken already. Try some work-around if this applies to you, but hopefully you can get the name you want! You will probably also want to use an email address associated with your domain, as well. This will not be a problem, since the domain is now yours and you can create as many email addresses as you want using it.

Once you have your brand secured across the web, email and social platforms, then you are officially in business. Congratulations! Can you believe that you are actually a real business entity? The total cost so far should be very low, definitely under $100. In most cases, the financial expense of these initial steps should be around $20 to $50. It would be virtually impossible to begin any other type of business for so little financial investment!

Now, you just have to actually start doing something to get the ball rolling on your new social influencer venture. All this conceptualizing and registering work is just the background to our business.

Now is where the real work begins! Are you ready? Remember, you will have to work really hard, so get used to the idea and learn to embrace it! Hard work is the way to the top of success mountain. Let's get climbing! Don't worry. I am going to tell you exactly what you need to do every step of the way. It's going to be a very exciting journey to be sure!

Part 2:
Getting Started as a Social Influencer

Which Social Platforms Should I Use?

Social media channels are always in flux. New platforms are continuously being created, while many older platforms are being phased out. The popularity of a social media platform can change virtually overnight. It is impossible to keep up with every trend in social media, since so many platforms just never live up to their hype and die off before gaining any real foothold in the vast marketplace of users.

So how do you choose which social media platforms to focus on? This can be a daunting question with no easy answers! Let's talk about your options for where to post your content...

Well established social media platforms are great because they are probably not going to disappear anytime soon (although they can i.e. Myspace, Google+). Large social networks provide many opportunities to connect with all manner of followers in any conceivable niche. However, well established platforms also have the most competition in terms of other influencers and advertisements already in existence.

Currently, the largest players in the social sphere are Facebook, Instagram, Twitter and YouTube. Other notable examples are Tiktok, Line, Pinterest, Whatsapp, Tumblr, SnapChat, ReddIt and StumbleUpon. There are countless less popular social networks, as well as tons of location-specific networks, especially for Chinese and other non-English speaking markets.

Most people who set out to become real professional influencers will focus on one or more of the primary social networks, including Facebook, Twitter, Instagram and/or YouTube. Each of these platforms is unique and provides features, benefits and drawbacks compared to its rivals. There is no objective "best" platform to become an influencer on. In fact, the majority of influencers who are very successful utilize multiple platforms simultaneously to reach more people, exert greater influence and distribute their content in different forms across the entire population of internet users.

In years past, some influencers chose to simply utilize their own websites to build their online empires, but now, this strategy is virtually unheard of. In order to become a real player in your industry, you really should utilize one or more of the main social networks, in addition to any web properties you develop on your own.

All of these social platforms have one major disadvantage that is obvious right from day 1 of use... No matter how hard you work and how successful you become, your fate on a platform is out of your hands, since you do not really control the content. The platform itself is the executor of your content and can decide, often quite arbitrarily, how they want to use it, promote it (or not) and whether it should be removed for any reason at all. Worse still, there is the possibility that after years of work investing in a specific platform, the network could lose all popularity, stranding your content or might even go completely out of business, removing you and everything you built from the internet forever... These are all VERY REAL risks and should be prepared for from the beginning of your influencer career. Failure to do so can spell disaster for you in the future, if the unthinkable occurs.

To this end, I universally recommend owning your content and paying to keep it online somewhere that you manage, such as on private hosting, a cloud server or on a secure storage platform. This is why every influencer should have their own website, although the benefits of having your own web space go far beyond this safety measure and will be discussed later in this book.

Furthermore, all photos, articles, posts, videos and any other work that you create must be kept on your own storage outside of your social network uploads. Simply uploading to a network and thinking the material will be safe there forever is idiotic. Additionally, the quality of the content is virtually always degraded on most current social networks, meaning that all your work which is actually seen will not be as good as the original version you created. Always keep your originals, even though this can mean investing in lots and lots of storage (particularly for video creators)!

So where do you start when it comes to choosing which social networks to focus upon? Let's look at the Big 4 and help you to decide!

Facebook is great because almost everyone already uses it and has a good idea how it works. Facebook allows you to communicate in words, pictures and video formats, making it very versatile for any influencer niche. Learning to use Facebook for business is simple and provides many opportunities to become a major influencer. However, Facebook also has lots of downsides to consider and seems to be losing popularity quickly compared to its competitors, especially among younger people. Industry insiders have declared Facebook to be "over" for several years already. However, it seems much more likely that the company will continue to evolve in response to changing trends and will most likely remain a powerful player far into the future.

Twitter has grown in popularity in recent years and is now a major influencer platform to rival any other. Twitter is a great way to engage people and build a following, but does have limitations about the type of content that can be delivered. Some people love Twitter, while others truly despise it. It is certainly one of the most polarizing of all social networks, to be sure.

Instagram (part of Facebook) is perfect for photographers, models, video creators and all manner of visual influencers. The platform has grown significantly and is one of the most popular now for building an influencer business. It is also still growing and considered well loved by most users, potentially giving it s bright future for many years to come.

YouTube is perhaps the most difficult social platform to succeed on, but remains one of the most profitable of all platforms for influencers who can build their channel, attract sponsors and utilize effective advertising solutions. YouTube has created many multi-millionaires, but now features a tremendous level of competition, making it harder than ever to break in and distinguish yourself as a content creator. Worse still, it is owned by Google, making it susceptible to dramatic algorithm changes on a regular basis. If you CAN make it on YouTube, you will be able to springboard yourself very far in the world, potentially entering into many complementary industries.

Smaller social platforms are less competitive, but also have fewer users and weaker prospects for a sustainable future. Business sectors tend to be dominated by a few major companies that own and control everything in established industries. Both Facebook and especially Google have been known to buy up any and all serious competition. This trust mentality is presently under scrutiny by many governments and hopefully will be broken up to allow more platforms to exist without all being part of the same parent-controlled organizations.

As mentioned previously, investing years of time in a platform only to have it disappear is every influencer's worst nightmare. Even if you can move your content, you must start all over from day 1. This is why I insist that multiplatform is the only way to go if you are serious about becoming a really successful social influencer.

My advice? Do Facebook, Instagram and Twitter for sure. Add YouTube if you can create engaging video content or are willing to pay someone to do it for you. Make sure to develop your own website (no, websites are not dead) and store all your content on your own managed devices or platforms to prevent any other entity from controlling where and how it gets used (or not). These are absolute necessities to get started as a serious influencer!

Total cost for accomplishing all of these things is generally zero. Joining any of the major social networks is free. You can invest in storage for your content as you go, since these tech products are easily scaled to meet your specific needs.

Build Your Website

NOW is the time to build your website. Don't wait. So many influencers make this mistake and simply put up a placeholder page and never get back to actually establish their brand. Not having your own website is unprofessional and will reflect poorly on you in the eyes of companies who might want to work with you. You will also have no self-managed place to share your work, making all your posts the property of another company on whatever social network they live on...

A good quality website will speak volumes about your brand, professionalism and commitment to becoming an influencer. Since you have the time now, create a website that will grow with you and sell people on your brand even when you are sleeping.

The work you invest learning and designing aspects of your website are very helpful skills moving forward for everything else you need to do anyway as an online influencer. You can create a logo and graphics that represent you and your new business and reuse these designs across all your social media channels. You can also work to create tag lines and business ideas on your website to guide your future social shares online across all your platforms. Simply becoming more adept at all things related to web design, hosting and other internet business needs will assist you in the coming months and years of your influencer career. If you know about these things already, then you have a big advantage! If not, then you need to start learning right now... If not, you will be paying people from this day forward to accomplish the most basic tasks for you and the cost will rise as your success grows.

You certainly do not have to have a perfect fully-featured website on day 1. Just start with something professional looking and simple, then work on it a bit each day. I can create an amazing website in minutes, as I am a professional webmaster now for many, many years. You may or may not have these skills, but it is easier now than ever before to learn how to do everything online. Any knowledge you pick up on performing web work will be extremely valuable moving forward, so take time and commit yourself to the process of becoming competent.

I highly recommend using WordPress as a content management system. It is the industry standard for a reason and is open source. No one will own any part of your website except you. There are plenty of other content management options, but none are ideal. Most CMS basically sell you a stripped down version of what WordPress can do, except at a much higher cost and with limitations and stipulations that are not ideal for your new business. If you are good with coding websites, then you might not require a premade content management system at all. If you already have these design skills, then you can decide what works best for your needs. You already know what you are doing...

You can certainly pay someone to design a website for you. However, this path will cause you to pay them (and others) over and over again as changes and updates are necessary. It is far more economical and enlightened to develop basic web skills yourself and it is really very simple to do. There are tons of free tutorials on building websites and WordPress really makes it a breeze. It is an idiotic-proof process, so don't worry! Maybe you have some friends who can help and if not, you can certainly pay someone now to do the "heavy lifting" and invest time to learn the skills yourself as your business grows.

Many new social influencers have the notion that websites are not needed. They believe that websites are considered old and antiquated technology. While it is true that many of your followers might not see every update on your website, some people will. However, companies who are interested in doing business with you will certainly want to see what you are about and there is no better representation of who you are than on your own website. This is where your content and voice can ring out exactly how you design them. Trust me... a quality website is a very good investment and the cost is so low that there really is NO REASON not to create a super site and put your unique stamp on it for the world to see!

I have been designed, building and hosting websites since the early 2000s. All of my online projects have benefitted from the knowledge that I have accumulated working on my own websites. I have also saved tons of money by doing everything myself and can even choose to make money anywhere in the world easily by offering these web services to others, if I so choose. Internet skills are great to have!

So how do you start? Well. Don't get suckered into some website builder that is substandard and overly expensive. Let me provide you with some tips to get your website up quickly and perfectly:

- As mentioned above, I recommend using WordPress. Not WordPress.com, but WordPress.org. The software is free and is super easy to install on any hosting service.

- Invest in decent hosting. Shared business hosting typically costs about $5 per month and long-term contracts will often provide nice discounts. Always look for coupon codes and you can get your hosting for much less. There is no reason to invest in any expensive hosting upfront, since upgrading is fast, easy and free on virtually every quality host company. Do NOT invest in any hosting which does not utilize the industry standard cPanel format.

- Do not use a free theme with WordPress. Buy a theme that is safe and secure. You will have a much better experience. I like Genesis Theme, but there are many great ones. I had a terrible user experience with X Theme and recommend avoiding it like the plague!

- Keep your website running lean. Everything you add will drain your hosting resources, cost you more money and slow your site down. Optimize images for small file size and web-friendly format. Keep plug-ins to a minimum. I recommend a security plug-in, an SEO plug-in and backup plug-in and that's about it. Managing comments can be done with a plug-in also, but it is much better to do it manually to avoid collecting tons of spam on your website.

- Some of this advice might not be meaningful to you right now. In fact, it might seem like a completely foreign language. Don't worry. Once you get into the website building process, it will all make sense to you. I promise! Keep these tips handy and refer to them as necessary to make quality decisions when building your site.

- If you do hire someone to design your website, have them use these parameters, since they should still use the best practices that will work in your interest now and far into the future. If they don't, you will be the one paying more for additional resource use and the need to make changes as your site fails for various reasons.

- I have built and run dozens of websites over the years and have made all my money online for the past 15 years. The advice I am giving you is solid, so don't let some newbie designer talk you out of it to make themselves more profit or to do less work on your behalf. There is no need to pay high monthly fees, use expensive software or add tons of options to your site that will only slow it down and cause it to break. Keep it sleek and simple.

- On the topic of subcontractors... Many people who work on the web simply suck. They are talentless hacks and terrible human beings. They are scammers, lazy and have little knowledge. In fact, if they work for you, they will cut corners at every opportunity to make things easier for them without regard your business or your future. Be careful when hiring subcontractors, since in my experience, about 70% of them simply suck and at least 50% are scammers in some form...If you find someone good to work for you, take care of them and pay them fairly. Also avoid any web worker who subcontracts out their jobs. They are simply middle men who are costing you more money than you need to spend. Cut them out of the deal!

Part 3:
Building Your Brand

What is Content?

Alright. Now you have your niche. You have your brand. You have your brand name registered on the web and across all the important social networking platforms. You have a shiny new website that makes you look like a pro. You are ready to grow your fledgling business! What do you do now???

Let's get you started on building content and influence. This IS your business model and will be the most important thing you learn in this book!

Content refers to your words, images, video and ideas. Anything that you create and share on your own website, on any other website, or on any social media channel, is considered content. It is the stuff that fills the internet and makes up the vastness of the web.

All your content should reflect who you are and what your brand is about. Building content is a strategic endeavor. It should never be haphazard or approached casually. You MUST create a consistent message and brand image if you are to have any hope at all of becoming successful as an influencer. This is a rule set in stone!

People want you to stand for something. You need to give them what they want and not deviate from your brand concept. Even a small degree of wavering from your usual POV might destroy months or years of work. So let's move into lesson one this topic below... Consistency!

Start Building with Uniformity

Uniformity means consistency. You must be consistent. Being an influencer is about finding new ways of sharing a consistent message over and over again. The more creative you are in being able to express your core brand image consistently, the more it will actually become you and you will become it. You want people to be able to recognize your content even without looking that it was you who created it. This is the mark of an expert influencer!

From day one, begin your brand with this goal in mind. Begin to establish your brand and talk about who you are, what you do and WHY you do it. WHY is it important to you? You must open yourself up to the experience of sharing yourself, as well as your niche, and begin to build authority early on in your business. If you fail in this objective, you will inevitably become a follower, instead of a leader. This is the nature of social media.

Start from the very beginning. Talk to people in clear language or with images or moving pictures. Remember that many, many people who see your posts do not speak your language, so be very cautious about the words and images you utilize, so that they do not get the wrong message from your posts!

Use words and images creatively. You must find your voice in order to reach people. If you sound like everybody else, you will be speaking constantly, but nobody will be listening. You need to be unique and find a way of communicating that literally shakes people awake to pay attention.

Be confident and be creative in all that you do. Use artistic expression, knowledge, experience, humor and any other tools that will give your work added appeal. Never be boastful, self-centered or entitled in your approach. There are influencers who embrace these shallow attributes, but they are typically just as hated as loved and tend to attract followers who are equally hated and therefore do not make good candidates for working with quality companies and other brands. Be humble and nice. It is not hard to do. I highly recommend it!

Every day, work on providing your audience greater insight to your brand and what you are all about. Over time, you will formulate a very complete picture of your brand for all to see and appreciate. You don't have to give away everything right from day one. Focus on adding some new thing about you or your brand every day. You will slowly paint a picture of your brand and if you do it right, the image created will be beautiful to your audience and they will naturally want to follow you. More importantly, the image created will be very appealing to companies that want to see you as their face, their voice, their representative, and are willing to pay you to be those things.

Want to get that kind of support? Then start now by creating your brand with consistency from day one and making it absolutely appealing and positive! While universal appeal is virtually impossible, try to attain it! Speak to everyone who will listen and try to convert them to followers, unless they pose a problem for you...

Don't let people shake who you are or who you want to be. There will be haters, hecklers and trolls. You will probably meet them very quickly. They will make you want to quit working online sometimes, but they can be handled professionally. Lets' go into some basics about dealing with these difficult types right now to prevent you from having to suffer under their whim once you begin posting content! The more you know who you are and what you are all about, the less people can negatively affect you with their cynicism, jealousy, ignorance and hate.

Dealing with Haters

As I mentioned previously, you will need to develop a thick skin in order to become a successful influencer. You will need to learn how to manage troublesome people and situations on your various social channels. You can not afford make mistakes in this regard.

If you handle things the wrong way, you will leave indelible evidence of your error for all to see and document. There is no way to be free of your social mistakes on the internet... Someone will always know and preserve what you did and share it. Therefore, be wary and cautious as you step into the domain of haters, trolls and various miscreants. If you lash out at them the wrong way even once, your own negativity might just put your new influencer career in jeopardy right from the start.

Haters will find you and try to make you miserable practically from day one. It seems inevitable that people must find a way to harass others online, so be prepared to deal with it:

- What should you do when a person is rude?

- Makes inappropriate comments?

- Sends inappropriate private messages?

- What about when a person contradicts your point of view, disagrees with you or corrects something that you stated as being an error?

These are a variety of scenarios that are commonly seen by social influencers when they begin posting.

It may take minutes or it may take weeks, but eventually, you will have to deal with people who are trying their very best to ruin your good time and sabotage your new business in the process. It really does not matter which social network you are using. The idea is that it IS social and will give people the opportunity to interact with you. When people are nice, this interaction can be so amazing! However, when they are mean, then you can feel very bad about yourself, your new business and people in general. What should you do when things go badly?

As far as people who do not agree with you or contradict you, you should accept their opinion and even thank them for it, as long as they are not rude or damaging in any way. People do not have to agree with you and you will earn lots of respect by understanding this truth and embracing it.

If someone points out an error you have made, then give them the benefit of the doubt and check it for yourself. If they are right, then thank them very sincerely for correcting you and tell them that you will be more careful in the future. Take the opportunity to connect with this person, if possible. They might become a mentor or ally to you. Owning your mistakes is an important part of personal growth and is crucial for anyone who wants to work on social networking platforms.

What about the rude, mean and inappropriate people? Some are just nasty and want a reaction from you. Some are perverts and will use sex as a weapon against you, especially if you are female. (Being a female influencer will leave you a target for pervs all over the world. Get used to it and learn to protect yourself ASAP or you will not last long in this business!) Some people are racist, sexist or otherwise prejudiced and want a forum to spread their hate. Some are just complete assholes. There is just no other way to put it! If they message you privately or post their hate on your profile or post, just block them on your social channels. This way they can not message or post to you anymore. This will not prevent them from talking about you on their own profile or posts, but who cares... Let haters do what they want. You do not need to be part of it. Never get in an argument with them. Never try to correct them. Never play along with them. These people will never be real friends or followers. They are a cancer on the web. They exist for one reason and one reason only... To make everyone else as miserable as they already are. Banish them to internet oblivion and move on. Don't take it personally!

If you can do this without emotional reaction, then all the better. I repeat. DO NOT TAKE IT PERSONALLY. If you do, you will burn out doing this work and learn to hate people, more than like them. This I promise you. Don't stress yourself. Learn to laugh off the haters and you will see that their negativity bounces off you harmlessly. You will become bulletproof. Your peace of mind and self-esteem will thank you!

Learn to recognize time-wasters quickly! It will not be difficult. These people do not actually engage your posts. They are merely after satisfying their own desires with you, often of a sexual or financial nature. They are typically really into you for no reason way too quickly. They talk to you non-stop. They are obvious predators. You just have to learn to read the signs and see them for what they are. You are here to get across YOUR agenda. Remember that! If they want to waste your time with theirs, then simply block them from your social platforms and move on. People who disregard your requests or message you constantly and aggressively should be immediately blocked. Do not engage these people. Do not argue with them. They will suck the life and energy out of you and give you a very bad attitude about your social influencer business. Just block them and move on as if they do not exist. After all, in your newly created internet universe, they don't! Good bye and good riddance!

Start Posting on Schedule

You should find a posting schedule that works for you and stick to it. Consistency is one of your greatest weapons on the way to be a successful influencer. I am shocked at how inconsistent some influencers are in their posting schedule and this unpredictability ALWAYS costs them exposure.

How often should you post?

This is a great question and it really depends on you, your niche and your followers' reactions. If you post just right, you will keep people engaged and satisfied. If you post too little, people will naturally seek to get their social fix from someone else... i.e. your competition. If you post too often, you will become a huge annoyance and very few people will actually follow you. You will be overexposed and your constant inane ramblings will make people run from you.

Find balance. Post quality content every time. EVERY TIME. NO EXCEPTIONS. The more often you can post quality content, the better, as long as you have something relevant to say and people are actually listening. This is a good general rule of thumb.

I personally can't stand when influencers post too infrequently or too often (even worse!) Try to find a nice schedule that serves both you and your followers. This is the key to true and profitable consistency on the web!

I tend to post every day, once a day, on my major social platform. I tend to post 1 to 3 times a week on less important social platforms and on platforms which require much more time commitment to create content, such as YouTube. I do not ever want to be a missing person to my followers, but I also do not want to become a bother or a bore...

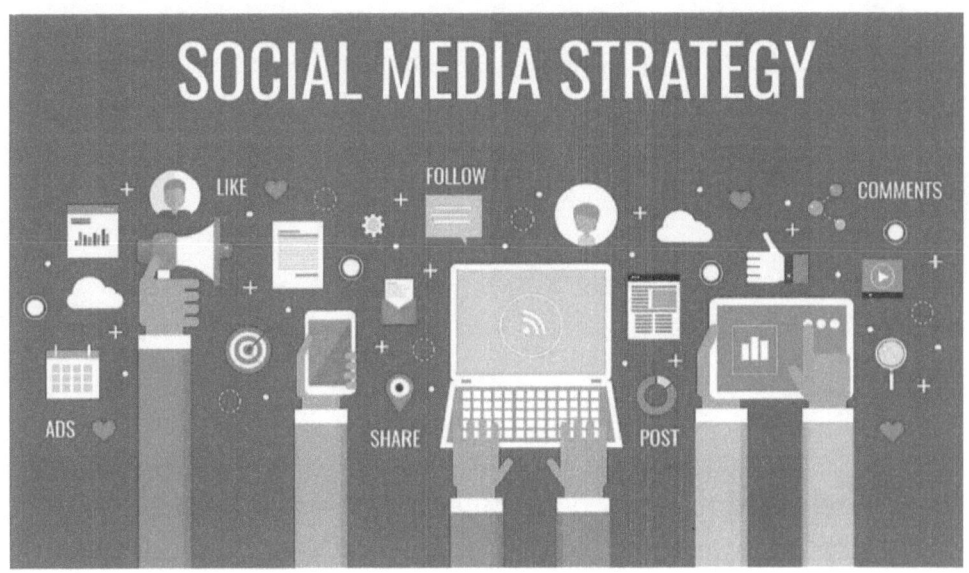

Commit to Your POV

Ok, so your brand is named and your internet presence is up and running. You are posting regularly on your preferred social channels and starting to get some attention from people who like your work. Some of these people will try to influence you to embrace their POV or to change direction for one reason or another. You must hold fast to your chosen niche and brand image unless YOU consciously decide to change it proactively for some reason.

Always remember your brand image and point of view when making any post on any social channel. Never go on autopilot and post something that does not work with your brand. Never post any content that does not mesh well with your brand image or philosophy.

If you are not steadfast in your direction, you will falter and fall by the wayside in terms of career progression. I have seen many promising influencers lose everything they have built by posting something that would be considered stupid by objective standards.

Never be sexist, racist, ignorant, biased, clueless, vengeful or unsympathetic. If you do, there will be consequences... now or eventually!

It is fine to expand your horizons as you move forward and offer more details about you and your life. In fact, I highly encourage you to personally connect to your followers. You are more than just your brand. Everyone understands this. However, when you do deviate from the usual course, make sure that you keep your eye on the brand image and only share personal things that are complementary to your point of view. If something stands out in contrast to what you claim to believe in, then you will not be authentic or convincing in anything you do from that moment forward. Therefore, think about every post twice before hitting that share button!

Remember that you can always go deeper into your niche and provide ever greater detail on specific aspects of your expertise. You do not have to talk about things outside of your immediate POV at all, if you choose not to. You simply do not have to engage followers on other topics or share anything personal about yourself. Lots of very successful influencers stick to one thing and one thing only. If they are not talking about that thing, then they are not talking at all. It is that simple... Other influencers are very open to sharing many facets of their life and thoughts that fall outside of their niche focus. However, they make sure that the things they share are still in harmony with the public persona they have created and are promoting every day as a professional social influencer.

The lesson here is to think carefully before posting. Never share without forethought and always consider the impact of your posts well in advance. If you can not exercise the self control and discipline to do this and feel that you have to share everything, then social influencer success will be even harder to attain for you than for the average person. It is best to develop good habits that protect you and your new brand from any harm; especially self-harm! This is why so many successful influencers take time to plan all of the posts far in advance and make sure that their shares will all be in harmony with each other, as well as meshing well with the general POV they are trying to convey. You really can not plan too much in this regard...

Build Content to Support Your POV

One of the major problems I see with new influencers is that they document everything that is going on in their lives and focus on the big events and special occasions that are meaningful to them. However, not all of these events and occasions are relevant to the brand image or POV of the influencer.

When I ask people why they shared a particular post or set of posts that seem very irrelevant to their carefully selected brand image, they always say the same things:

"I just needed a post."

or

"I am out of content that represents my brand right now, so I just used this..."

Never let this happen to you. Take time to plan your posts and actually create content that is not organically occurring in your life. This is called post orchestration and can be a very important strategy. In essence, you will create the post by first creating the situation, then documenting it. I can not tell you how many people try to find situations to document and share, but never think to actually create the situations that would best serve their brand POV!

Need content? Make it! Life is not cooperating to provide what you need? Give it some help and make the situation exist so that you can document it and share it. This is why you need to be creative.

Being an influencer is about crafting yourself and your brand. You MUST create the life that you want. You must find a way to be engaged in scenarios on a day-to-day basis that will support your brand image and POV. If you are not active in actually doing what you talk about, then you have zero credibility and should quit right now or get busy trying harder...

Go out and do. Document. Share. Repeat! This is the formula for social influencer success. There is no other way.

Let's look at some examples. An influencer wants to share her thoughts on the latest fashions in her area at a given time. She goes out with her camera and voice recorder each day for a week trying to get some awesome images of cool looks and recording her thoughts as she does this. However, she finds that she can not achieve this goal. No one around her is wearing what she considers cool or hip for the season. Maybe the weather is not cooperative. Maybe she is looking in the wrong places.

Instead of going on day after day without building any content and feeling very discouraged, this newbie influencer should just document herself wearing the looks that she wants to showcase. This way she is creating the situation purposefully and then has the ease of documenting it in completely controlled conditions! She could just as easily make the situation seem completely organic by recruiting some friends to dress-up in some carefully selected outfits and then following them throughout their day to document them and people's reactions to them.

It is awesome if you can just observe life and get all the content you need. However, when life disappoints and does not fully cooperate, you will find that a bit of planned ingenuity is the perfect answer for any lack of content. Just create what you want, how you want to do it, even if it means planning the entire thing down to the smallest detail.

To this end, you will find many travel influencers planning every moment of every post campaign around the ability to document the things they want to showcase. Travel influencers will carefully plan their trips to ensure optimal post opportunities. They will choose where they go, what they do, and when they do it based on ideal content creation conditions. As an established travel influencer, this is the life I live and have done so for a long time now!

You will find tech influencers making sure to be at every event and device launch to have immediate access to products as they materialize in the consumer marketplace. Many will even do whatever it takes to get advance products before they are released to the general public.

Lifestyle influencers create an entire day's worth of activities just so that they can get the perfect post. This is pure creativity combined with dedication, problem solving and a take-charge attitude that will help any influencer in any niche to succeed. As a benefit, the influencer gets to live life exactly as they choose and do what they love to do!

The point is that every type of influencer must go above and beyond what they think they can do in order to truly become influential in their niche. The best way to accomplish this goal, whatever the niche might be, is to be incredibly active in your endeavor. Work hard, network, and always have your mind on what type of content can be created in every situation. Being an influencer is NOT a 9 to 5 job. There is no time off! You must be working to some degree all the time in order to stay current and stay relevant!

Plan Ahead in Content Creation

One of the most common of all mistakes made by influencers is falling behind in content creation. It is an absolute necessity to have content ready at all times and more content should always be available than is ever needed at a given time. In essence, always have spare posts ready to go, just in case you need them.

Failing to have content prepared forces many influencers to release posts that are not finished, not appropriate, low quality or not brand-serving. No post should ever be released unless it is perfect! PERFECT. Content is made to serve a specific purpose. If you release content just because you feel that you MUST and have nothing solid created, then the compromise post will fail and you will eventually fail, as well.

Therefore, take time to create content that is timeless and can be released at any time a post is needed, but not ready. Problems happen that can derail any planed social post or campaign. If you are prepared, the audience might get something unexpected, but at least it will be a post of high value and relevancy. This can only be guaranteed if you create extra content and store it until it is actually needed.

Some content creators go live, vlog every day or practice some similar impromptu circumstance. They feel that because of their chosen social influencer model, they NEVER have to create content in advance. This might work as long as everything goes perfectly for them, but guess what... Eventually something will derail their day's share and they will have no back-up available. No matter what type of social sharing you do, ALWAYS have a backup post available. In fact, you should have many!

When I am working, I always have at least one extra YouTube video ready to go. I write my blog content far in advance and routinely have 20 to 100 posts written and edited at any time for publication as required. Instagram photos are a primary social share for me, so I usually have at least 3 to 4 months ready at all times, since I post every day. After large and important trips, I might have up to 6 months of picture posts ready to share!

I never have to settle or share something that is mediocre. I can always post something awesome and my followers appreciate it! You must follow this same guidance if you want to minimize stress for yourself when something goes wrong and your scheduled post is not available to be shared. Be prepared to have a plan B, C and D to implement, just in case... You can never have too much prepared content, but you can certainly have too little to share.

Offer Value

What will make people follow you, instead of following someone else? What will make them continue to follow you once the initial "love affair" period ends? The most important part of follower attraction and retention is the idea of providing value to your supporters. In essence, you need to offer them something that helps them in some way consistently and makes their life better.

You might be able to provide services, knowledge, inspiration, deals or just pure entertainment. However, if you are to build a successful influencer business, you will definitely need to offer something and preferably, many different things of value. The more you can give, the more you will get back in terms of follower growth and retention!

To this end, when designing posts, always think to yourself: "What value am I giving with this post?" If the post is self-serving, the only person who will truly relate to it is you. Therefore, you must find your voice and sell yourself to the audience by offering them something that resonates with THEM. This is a great continual process of denying the needs of your own ego in favor of providing for the common good:

- So what value can you provide?

- Can you make this value proposition work every day?

- Can you be consistent day after day in your offerings?

- Will you get tired of giving?

You better have the right answers to these questions or you are surely going to falter in your new business. You must give until it hurts, then give some more...

If you have experience in a particular thing, you already have the opportunity to share your knowledge and provide outstanding value in the way of facts, opinion and creative editorializing of the subject matter.

If you are an artist of some sort, you can share your work, be it painting, video, photography or music and allow your art to speak volumes on your behalf.

You can partner with companies and offer special discounts on products and services. Everyone loves a discount and if you are the one providing it, then you have immediately made yourself important and added value to your brand.

You must be very careful with your value proposition. Many influencers partner with dubious companies that offer a small discount using a specific coupon code which is assigned to the influencer. The influencer receives a percentage of money in some cases or simply can use the code in promotions in other cases. Regardless, the company might be very poor in terms of quality and ethics. The products or services they offer might be actually overpriced garbage. They are using the influencer to perpetrate consumer fraud on the public at large.

Be extremely careful who you partner with, since getting onboard one of these scam ships will have you sunk as an influencer in no time at all... Just because a company reaches out to you does not mean that they are a good fit for your brand. In fact, be wary of unsolicited partnerships, especially when you are new and up-and-coming in your new career path!

You can even provide value simply by being a critic. Review anything you want and share your thoughts with people who are looking for reviews from knowledgeable real people with real experience, just like you.

However, you need to do some very important things in order to differentiate your posts from the posts shared by just anyone: You need to build authority and build trust.

Build Authority

Why should people listen to you instead of just disregarding whatever you say or troll you right off the internet? They will listen if you can successfully build authority. Make yourself into a leader in your niche and people WILL follow you. You need to provide value, as we discussed before and you must learn to actually lead people. Doing this takes time and dedicated effort.

You can't just make a statement of your qualifications and expect anyone to listen or care. You must introduce your skills, knowledge and aptitudes to your audience over time and allow them to decide that you actually know what you are talking about. Telling them that you are knowable just sounds boastful and tends to make people think, "Who cares? What a jerk!"

You will stay consistent with your brand image and POV, sharing lots of posts about your focused niche. You will create authority by doing this alone, as long as your posts are consistently high quality and resonate with people.

Followers will come to associate you with what it is you do and if you do it well, then you will become the "go-to" person in that niche for that person. If you reach enough people and succeed in becoming the "go-to" person, then congratulations... You have now built a very lucrative influencer business!

When establishing authority, it is best to provide your point of view and invite interactions regarding your posts. If someone shares something of worth, be sure to thank them and integrate this thing into your future posts. If someone questions what you post in a negative way, you can easily fight back best using your knowledge and skills in your niche focus. Everyone likes when a person can defend their position with skills, rather than just emotion. In fact, if you can prove yourself right with dignity and grace, even the person who argued with you will likely come around to respect you. Need to establish authority? Be capable of debating your point openly, in a friendly manner and coming out on top. You will get respect from all who enjoy the post!

Simply being consistent with your posts day after day will establish authority in any niche. It is taken for granted that people who work in a given niche have knowledge related to that topic. When you build your brand over time and maintain a consistent POV, it will be virtually impossible for anyone to undermine your authority, since you will be offering value every day and showing yourself to be a person worthy of following to everyone who is exposed to your work.

When people step forward to defend you and your work without solicitation, you will surely know that you are doing something right. If you get hecklers on a daily basis without anyone coming forward to fight on your behalf, then you are doing something very wrong. Make adjustments as needed! Always be self-critical and look for ways to improve yourself and your business. Results are one of the best measures of your progress on the path to success!

Build Trust

Building trust is similar to building authority in that you can't force it to happen. If you simply come out and tell people, "Trust me", their gut instinct will likely be the opposite! They will probably doubt anything and everything you will share... It is far better to allow them to test you in their own way and to earn their trust over time with the consistent value proposition of your posts.

Trust is one of the most important commodities for any influencer. It will get you through times of challenge and allow you to embrace financially beneficial opportunities that will raise the value of your brand exponentially.

If people like you, like what you are saying, like your work and are interested in your niche, then trust will naturally follow. Just don't demand it or rush it. Everyone has their own timeline to establish trust and some people might respond faster than others. Just keep at your work with your goal on consistency and value each day and your followers' trust will open many doors for you.

Engage and Interact

What is engagement and what is interaction? While these things might seem similar or even identical in some people's minds, they are actually unique and equally important to the future success of your influencer business.

Engagement means to capture the attention of your audience. They will see your posts and take time to look at them, instead of just allowing them to pass into the abyss of their feed, never to be seen again. How do you engage people? There are a million answers to this question, depending on exactly what it is you do.

All of your posts should be designed to engage! Capture people's attention and fight for your share of time on your favorite social platform. Utilize a combination of powerful words, images and video content to engage people who already follow you, as well as people who will see your work for the first time. This takes some degree of skill, since you want EVERY post to be capable of engaging new and old audience members alike. With time and practice, you will see what works for you by studying user engagement metrics and understanding what parts of your game still need work.

The best way to optimize engagement is simply by doing everything that I have outlined above on a consistent basis, as well as by adding visual and/or audio flare to every one of your posts. In essence, make them look, sound and feel amazing! Make your posts resonate with people. This basically means that your content consistently strikes a personal, emotional chord. People will be able to "see themselves" in your words and images.

This is where your special creativity comes into play. Remember that if you want to be a successful influencer, the best path towards that success is you and your skills. Build them. Share them. Impress with them. Captivate with them! Do it every day and you will climb that mountain to the pinnacle of social success over time.

Interaction means to communicate directly with people who see your posts. People might want to publicly comment on you or your work. They might want to message you privately to get information or learn more about you. Many followers will do both on a regular basis. You need to find the right approach to interacting with your followers in a way that suits you, your niche, your followers' needs and practicality. This is a skill that many influencers struggle with and here is why...

A common problem is that you are "too busy" to answer all the messages and comments you get. What happens in these cases is that people you ignore tend not to message or comment ever again.

"You ignore me. I ignore you".

You lost your influence on these people and can not bring them closer to you in your circle of followers. Every message and comment is an opportunity to gain a solid follower for life. It just takes developing an approach that will allow you to find time to perform these important interactions, while not negatively impacting the other vital and time-consuming tasks involved in your social influencer business.

Another common problem is the desire to interact constantly with everyone and engage in all manner of side conversations privately. This is a very bad idea. There are only so many hours in a day and you can not use all of them discussing things with individual followers one-by-one. They will ask you for "only 10 minutes of your time", but when you have tens or hundreds of thousands of followers, this will amount to more hours than are available each day and you will accomplish little to nothing by interacting with them privately during this time.

Basically, you will be spinning your wheels and going nowhere, while simultaneously being exhausted by working so long and so hard to get nowhere... I strongly suggest limiting the time you spend privately discussing anything with anyone, outside of collaborations, personal friends and business ventures.

You must develop a strategy that allows you to keep people interested in you, while still sparing yourself the time commitment of engaging each person individually. You must engage your entire audience all together and use a very small amount of time to show each follower some personal attention. This is a crucial balancing act and it can become really problematic as your business grows!

I tend to advise most influencers to create a basic message to share with people who contact just to chat with you. Chat is the destroyer of productivity. You WILL NOT have time to chat. This message will essentially say:

Thank you for contacting me. I really appreciate your support. I am very friendly and engaged with my followers who comment publicly on my posts. However, I use this private messaging space for my work only. Therefore, please only talk to me in the public comments.

This approach tends to work well to reasonable followers without putting people off too much. Just be sure to actually acknowledge every comment by liking it or replying to it, if not both. If you ignore a comment, you will likely not get another from the same person and even others will see your indifference and probably not comment either. People who do not respect this message will tend to be problematic anyway, so feel free to simply ignore their private messages from that moment onwards. As I mention before, some people are just more trouble than they are worth.

There is much more to be said on the subjects of engagement and interaction. You will need to navigate these important topics very carefully and find an approach that works best for you. You will know how well your strategy is working by your results and business growth.

There is no point working really hard to gain new followers if you are steadily losing old followers. You need to achieve the right balance of engagement and interaction, while still allowing yourself time to do everything else that is needed in your life. You can not become a slave to your device to chat with everyone all the time and expect to achieve success. You will have no time to actually create content or do anything else for that matter!

Tips on Interacting with Followers

It is really important that you have personalized interactions with people who show interest in your work. However, this can be a very daunting proposition as your business grows, since you might have tens of thousands, hundreds of thousands or even millions of people following you and YOU are just one person! Therefore, take advantage of the time when you have few followers to get to know the ones you do acquire!

If you can make a connection to a person and establish authority and trust as noted above, then you will likely have a follower for life, unless you do something to ruin it. In order to make this valuable connection, here are some of my top tips when it comes to interacting with people who see and appreciate your work:

Find common ground. You probably can find something about each person that connects you. Highlight this thing in your interactions with the person and they will feel a bond forming between you over a shared interest, attribute or experience.

Refer back to your bond when you relate to each person. Develop good memory skills to remember what each person is about or check their profile quickly before responding to them to refresh your memory. Checking also gives you a chance to interact with their newest content, so this strategy is strongly advised when time allows.

Positive public interactions build your brand, so encourage them. As noted above, talking to people privately does nothing to help you. Move the conversation public and you will find that people will behave better and add value to your brand with their appreciation of your work. You will also lose 99% of the creeps who perv out when talking privately.

When you begin to recognize the type of person that wastes your time, simply block them immediately. Do not waste time with people who continue to disregard your request not to contact privately or people who are inappropriate in any way. Do not engage in side conversations that are unproductive. It might feel like a defeat to lose a follower, but trust me, in the long-run, these people are ALWAYS more trouble than they are worth. Weed them out quickly and spare yourself more trouble. Good bye and good riddance to parasites of all sorts!

All this being said, try to make each follower feel special at least occasionally. Keep that connection strong with positive reinforcement as time allows. A small effort can go along way, especially as your grow in influence. Your little actions will mean more once people see and understand how busy you really are...

Shares

Sharing is one of the best ways to interact on any social media platform. Sharing can help you to assist others in growing their audience or encourage your followers to pay attention to a particular person, company, offer, product or service. It is great if you can share relevant content on your social platforms, since it will add to the number of quality posts you can offer and will continuously engage your audience productively. Sharing content is a great way to get others to share your content in return and can also be an excellent income stream.

However, getting people to share your content is your main priority when trying to expand your social influencer business. Each share will give your post new life, allowing it to reach more people than it could on your profile alone. If you receive a high quality share from a larger influencer or commercial page, then your reach could grow exponentially in a very short time!

How can you encourage sharing? Let's look at some of the best practices that will make others want to share your content on their own pages:

- You can simply ask people to share! "Sharing is caring" sentiments can go a long way with your real fans. Get in the habit of asking for shares, since many of your followers might forget about the power they have to share your content!

- You can offer compensation or some mutually beneficial arrangement to other influencers who share your content. This can be a complicated arrangement, since the cost must be worth the exposure or you will consistently end up losing money to make small gains, if any at all, in your business valuation.

- You can reach out to large niche pages that only share other people's content. (They do not create content of their own). These "super consolidator" pages often have huge audiences, despite offering no real value. Yes, they piss me off, since they make money like parasites without any creative process, but they seem to be here to stay, so you might as well learn to use them to your benefit.

Tagging

Tagging is a great way to increase the reach and engagement metrics of your posts. Tagging means to name another person or entity in the post using their user name or hashtag. Why would you want to name another person or entity in your posts? There are several reasons...

The first reason for tagging is to allow more people to see and interact with your posts. Simply put, tagging a person or entity immediately calls attention to the post and on many social platforms, the content will now also appear on the profile of the tagged person or entity, offering you exposure to their audience, as well as your own.

The next reason for tagging is to fulfill collaboration agreements, such as naming the people you worked with when creating a post or simply to provide some exposure for your friends or regular collaborators. Simply tagging each other regularly can harness the power of 2 separate profiles to assist each influencer in building a larger and more engaged audience.

Finally, tagging can be done in order to fulfill a commercial agreement, such as when running a sponsored post or a series of sponsored posts, called a campaign. The influencer can tag the sponsor or their products in the post in order to call attention and potentially cause the user to engage with the tag, opening up a possibility for commercial gain.

Tagging is a great tool and should be utilized often and creatively. However, when abused, tagging becomes worthless and can actually be counterproductive. Here are some tagging best practices:

- Tag conservatively. No one likes a post with hundreds or thousands of people tagged within it.

- Do not tag arbitrarily. Only tag a person or entity when the post actually relates to them or if they helped to create it or sponsor it.

- Make sure to use the correct tags! You would be amazed how many people mis-tag their posts, sending traffic to a page that does not deserve any credit. This happens because many people create profiles with names which are incredibly similar to the actual person or entity which is desired to be linked-to via tagging. Be very careful that you do not help these lazy scammers to build their businesses at your expense!

- You DO NOT need to tag yourself in posts. It's actually really stupid and annoying!

- Encourage your followers to tag their friends in your posts! This is a great way to increase your reach and call attention to your post with a new audience each day. You can also encourage followers to tag themselves in your post if they "like it" or agree with whatever message you are trying to get across to them.

You must find effective ways to get people and pages to share your content and tag you as much as possible if you want to grow. If not, then your pace will slow and other influencers will outwork you and make it up the mountain much quicker. You must leverage all the help you can get when building your brand. Sharing and tagging are 2 great tools to learn to exploit!

You Must Be the Hunter

In order to become successful as a social influencer, you MUST make a proactive effort to connect with new people continuously. You CAN NOT just create content and wait for the world to come to you, especially now in the days of algorithm changes that can bury you and your business at the bottom of a seemingly endless list of influencer posts in a day.

You must hunt for followers and do so by engaging them and interacting with them. You must show initiative! If you can make the initial effort and show interest in them, they will likely respond and give your posts a look. If you are doing your job well, you will captivate them and they will join your most loyal followers.

You do not have to spend money to gain new followers or get more exposure for your posts, although many influencers do invest cash in promotions and advertising with varying results... You will need to invest time and effort in this process and will once again have to develop a thick skin in order to manage the common incidence of being rejected in your attempts to connect with new people.

If you have ever held a cold-calling job, you will have an advantage here. Finding new followers is a lot like "cold calling". You need to find an "in" to connect with people who you do not know and who do not know you in return. You need to find that "common ground" I spoke about earlier and use it to break the ice... If you can foster a connection, then the rest of the relationship will fall naturally into place and you will grow in your influence.

Remember all of our previous lessons here. You will need to find some way of interacting with lots of new people every day, without it taking up all of your time. I normally recommend liking some of their posts and adding comments that reflect your brand POV. Find common ground with people any way that you can. Look for something that you might have in common and use that thing to make a connection with them.

Similarly, look out for people who will obviously not be a good fit for you or your brand. Some people post things on their social media which immediately excludes them from my interests. I actually go so far as to block these people as soon as I discover them so that I do not make additional effort in the future trying to connect with them and I will certainly not pay to promote a post that might be put in front of their eyes. They are a bad fit for me and I do not want them as part of my follower base. If a social platform gives you the ability to block undesirable people, learn how to do it quickly! Blocking is one of your greatest tools to save effort, time and money.

Once you get new people following you, make absolutely sure to continue to reconnect with them to some degree on a regular basis. The biggest mistake some influencers make is to ignore the posts of their followers and cause their fans to view the relationship as extremely one-sided. Basically it is all work for the follower and all benefit for the person they are following. It needs to be a two-way street to some degree, so make some effort and give something back to each person when you can. Liking some posts and making some comments can go a long way to keeping a relationship authentically close and making your followers feel appreciated, as well as intimate.

Go Get Followers

Most social networks will provide suggestions for connecting with people who might be interesting to you. These suggestions may be based on mutual acquaintances, mutual interests, similar location, language or many other factors. In my experience, many of these suggestions are complete crap, while some are good matches. However, all suggestions give you the opportunity to connect with a new person, so it is best to take as many chances as possible to form new relationships and grow your follower base.

One of the best ways to find followers is to harvest them from your existing fans. Most social platforms allow you to easily connect with people who are already connected to your followers. This is a great way to find people of similar mindset and a great way to convert one new follower into potentially hundreds for each new person you connect with.

The more followers you have, the more existing connections they will have. Therefore, this pool of prospective followers increases exponentially as your own follower-base grows! Best of all, this method of connecting with new people is absolutely free!

You can sometimes get good opportunities to connect with a large group of prospective followers on groups and on message boards that are similar in focus to your niche. If you can add value to the group or board, then other users will recognize this benefit and will tend to follow you without even being asked to do so.

Becoming a valued part of any online community will certainly go a long way towards making quality connections with others in that same community, so take time to research and interact with these resources often to expand your follower base. Finally, being an active leader on a message board or group with help you to establish authority, which creates the organic desire for people to follow you.

When you do anything in life, keep your eye out for chances to connect with people in the real world. Be prepared to say hi and offer a connection to them if the circumstances are right. Always promote your business in a way that is not aggressive and comes off as friendly and in the person's best interest.

I tend to gain many followers by simply talking to people in the real world and directing them to my social pages as the conversation allows. Of course, part of my conversational skill is to turn the topic of talk towards this goal and then deliver my message, which is almost universally warmly received. It is a subtle art, but it does not take long to figure out exactly how to do it for many different types of influencer niches. Since I am a healthy lifestyle and travel influencer, it is really very simple, since I can engage people on almost any topic. This makes my entry to the conversation very natural and well-intentioned. Part of my appeal is that I TRULY want to help people to live better and accomplish their goals. Having tangible sincerity is always a good attribute! People can get a real sense of what you are really about in person, so always have a polished and helpful approach when dealing with prospective followers in the real world! Let's discuss this topic in greater detail...

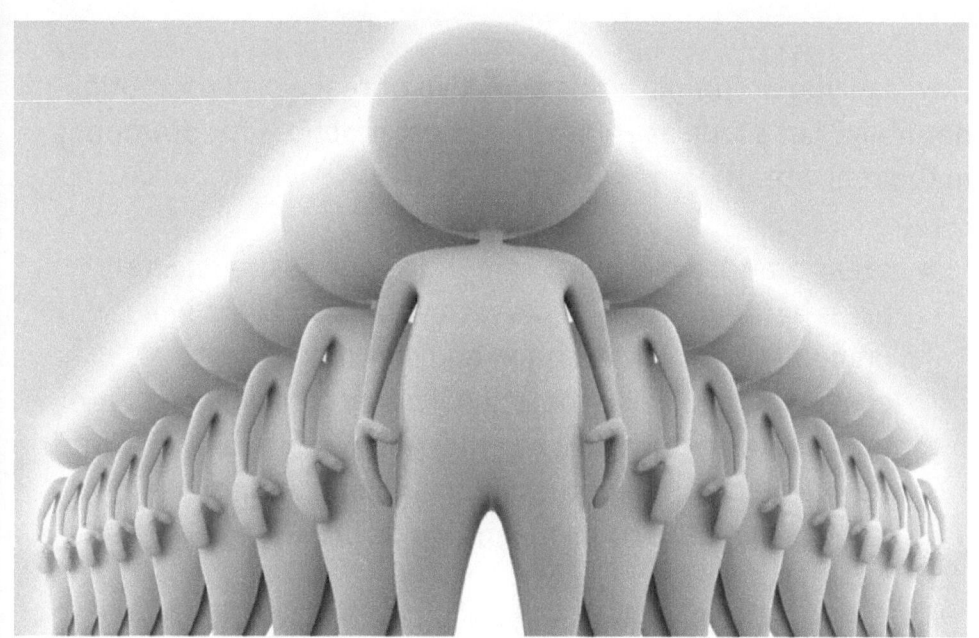

Real World Promotion

One of the biggest mistakes that new influencers make is leaving the real world out of their promotion strategy. They might work all day and night on promoting online, but refuse to even talk to anyone in the actual world about their business. This is madness and is completely self-defeating!

Connecting with real people in the real world is a great way to build your influencer business, especially if you have the chance to interact with them in a situation that is relevant to your niche.

I suggest integrating your brand and POV into your daily routine as much as possible. You do not have to beat your family and friends to death with your business. They are already your supporters. However, go out of your way to expose new people to you and your brand each and every day in everything that you do.

How can you accomplish this objective of real world promotion naturally? Let's look at some of the best practices for promoting in the real world:

- Wear branded clothing promoting your business. Shirts, bags, hats and other items with your brand logo will immediate attract attention and can start many conversations. This promotional benefit makes the cost of these items worthwhile many times over. If you can afford to give away some of these items to encourage free advertising, then by all means, go for it!

- Engage people whenever and wherever you can. Look for natural openings to introduce yourself and your brand, even if it is only in passing. If you patronize a business, leave a business card when you pay your bill or better yet, make up a second style of business card featuring a summarized version of your sponsorship options on the back.

- Use your official company name website and email when dealing with ANY organization or business. Simply switching from a personal email to your business email will expose many people to your brand. Additionally, create an interesting footer to your business email to provide some insight to your brand and POV.

- Try to create business accounts with all your vendors featuring your brand name. Business accounts often have additional benefits when compared to consumer accounts. You may need to officially register the company, which you should do anyway. Remember, you are building a real business here!

- Be careful not to sound self-important when interacting with people in the real world (or online for that matter). Instead, find ways to promote yourself organically without being boastful or self-serving in approach. A good way to strategize this is to put yourself in the other person's position and then find dialog which appeals to you and does not make you feel negatively towards the promoter. Fine tune your script ideas before using them in the real world!

Dealing with Language Barriers

Since social media is an international phenomenon and since you will likely benefit from having followers in more than one country, you will need some tools to help you to connect with people. It is absolutely necessary to use translation software, since many social networks have poor, sporadic or non-existent translating options. In most cases, I highly recommend posting and connecting with people in English, since this is a universal language, but this advice does not always apply and might be impossible for some influencers anyway, since they have little knowledge of this language. However, if you want to grow really big, English is certainly the way to go!

You already know that you will need good translation software on whatever social medial platforms you are utilizing. Some platforms offer translation, while others do not. Always be prepared to deal with questions and comments in other languages besides your own!

Remember too that many people might speak to you in a language that is not their native tongue. Therefore, when suspecting such a situation, try to communicate as clearly as possible in proper grammar and without slang in order to keep your meaning crystal clear. There are many possible problems stemming from the use of different languages and misunderstandings are commonplace. Always do everything you can to attempt to communicate clearly to your entire audience and do not utilize language that can be misunderstood, potentially causing insult or isolation.

This guidance is a tall order and you are bound to fail in this regard at some point. I have found many situations where people even misidentify the meaning of simple emojis. They will ask "Why are you laughing at me?" in response to a simple smiley face. Don't get rattled by such questions, as you can simply clarify your meaning in order to assuage any doubts and create a better feeling between you and any confused audience members.

You can certainly encourage people to speak to you in your own language and place the burden of understanding on them. However, this will certainly cause some people to simply lose interest and wander away, which might be a loss or a gain to your social presence, depending on how you look at it and the potential troubles language barriers might create for you.

Be warned that many social platforms offer limited or no translation for comments and personal messages. The platforms which do translate often provide poor quality results. Even the very best translation tools fail much of the time, especially with certain languages. Be warned that errors will occur. Be prepared and do not become confrontational over language issues. If the situation escalates, just block people who are causing more problems than they are worth.

Be Culturally Sensitive

In similar fashion, cultures are very different around the world and things which might be acceptable and even entertaining to some people might be incredibly demeaning, insulting or infuriating to others. As a global social influencer, it is best to maintain a culturally-sensitive and enlightened stance that will not make enemies of entire countries, religions, ethnicities or groups of any kind for that matter. You DO NOT want to become public enemy #1 of any demographic, since they will band together to make your life hellish.

I said before and will say it again, be confident in what you post. Do not take chances by posting things that could be detrimental to your career. If you make a serious social faux pas, your influencer career will go away almost instantly and might NEVER come back. There are no second chances for people deemed to be racists, bigots, prejudiced or otherwise sociopathic.

You can support or attack whomever you choose if it serves your brand and POV. However, do it fairly and objectively. Do not make things personal, since this will make you look immature, unprofessional and undesirable from a prospective sponsor's point of view.

People all have their sensitivities, so be wary of triggering them. You might not agree with everything you see and hear, but choose your battles wisely. Remember that your POV is very subjective and that others who share opposing ideals are not wrong. They are just different.

If you fight fairly, you will be respected, even by your potential enemies. If you resort to low blows and encourage conflict among people, your career as an influencer will only exist in a very limited capacity. You will become a messiah to trolls and other sociopaths and will not get very far. You certainly will not ever cross into mainstream success, so you might as well quit now... Just be wary, intelligent and try to embrace a global POV when making a post about anything.

Religion and politics are the 2 most polarizing topics. If you are going to comment on either, expect trouble justifiably. You caused the issue yourself as soon as you decided to provide commentary on these subjects!

Be Worthy of Your Followers' Support. Be a Leader

In order to be looked at as an icon in your niche, you must actually become a leader. While it is fine to follow trends when you are working on building your brand, established influencers are the ones actually creating trends and dictating how their niche is evolving in real time.

In order to reach the upper echelon of professional social influencers, you must become an innovator with a unique perspective that provides value to your followers.

How do you step into a leadership role? There are many things you can do to provide a resounding answer to this question! You might not have been born a leader, but in order to become a successful influencer, leadership skills are a MUST-HAVE! Let's delve into some ways that you can foster the skills that you will require to become a true leader in your niche:

- Provide your opinion on trends and how you would like to see things change or stay the same. Provide credible reasons to support your opinions to help sway your followers to embrace your opinion as an upcoming trend.

- Become ever-more deeply involved in your niche. Get to know all the important people who are interested in the same things as you. Network with these people and use your combined connections to benefit your brands. It is vitally important to earn respect and support from your peers if you want to have a smooth ascent in the influencer world. Too many people end up in feuds and conflicts that might add fuel to their fire in the short-term, but also help to burn them out in the long run.

- Help up-and-coming influencers in your niche and in related niches. Mentoring others is a great way to raise your own position by default. This is the same approach used for hundreds of years in martial arts training, where the master is recognized by consensus opinion of their students, rather than by self-proclamation.

- Use your influence to actually change your niche for the better. Partner with companies and organizations to spearhead your vision into tangible reality. Talking about things is great, but making them come to fruition is much better. Is there something you want preserved? Work to preserve it. Something you want changed? Work diligently to change it. Your voice is the most powerful weapon you have as an influencer, so make it heard loudly and often. Create and pursue short and long-term goals in this regard.

Be Careful Being a Critic

Some influencers have made careers being critical and even cynical. There is nothing inherently wrong with a critical perspective, but it can be a very negative experience to become trapped in. What does it mean to be critical? Well, this depends on the intention of the critic...

Some critics use there influence to improve their niche and the companies and products within that niche. They honestly share their positive and negative opinions in the hope of bringing positive change. They also want to help fellow consumers within their niche to differentiate truly great products and services from substandard offerings.

This form of critical POV is both honorable and can be highly profitable. By your critical assessment, you are offering value. You are showing people the upside and downside of whatever it is you are talking about so that they do not invest in it and then get a nasty unwanted surprise themselves. Basically, you are taking the financial fall for them and showing why a product or service is or is not acceptable.

Criticism simply for the sake of being mean, unrealistic in your expectations or just to propagate a continuous cynical atmosphere in your sphere of influence will generally lead to a short and miserable career. While some influencers seem to say and do whatever they want, including being overly-critical and cynical people, they rarely enjoy all levels of success in their business. They may make money, but frequently do so at the expense of their very soul. No one wants to be unhappy all the time! It is just not a nice path to travel...

Success Takes Time

How long will it take to succeed as a social influencer? This is one of the most common questions people ask before getting started on their own path. Unfortunately, there is no universal answer...

I have seen people achieve amazing success in a relatively short period of about a year's time. This fast ascent is not common, but is certainly possible given optimal circumstances.

Most serious influencers take about 3 years of fulltime effort to achieve a satisfying measure of success and recognition. They must work hard during this time and accept periods of plateau along the way as being part of the typical process.

Some influencers work hard for many years without ever breaking into the upper echelon of success. However, they do become known and use this notoriety to play the long game. Sometimes, the people who stand the longest eventually get recognized for their complete body of work and become highly regarded over time. I have seen many influencers never achieve the absolute heights of their niche, but last there much longer than people who have reached the top, but eventually disappear as quickly as they ascended.

If you never quit, then you can not lose. You should not be in a race for success, but instead working to fulfill your present goals every day. If you stay your path and continue to lay out your roadmap towards the pinnacle strategically day by day, success will eventually come, even if it is simply in the form of not failing...

Do not stress about how long you are working to achieve your goals. Just keep your vision in sight at all times and press forward. This is the way to success in all things in life, including those which seem to be impossible. If you quit, then you lose at that very moment. However, if you persevere, you are always leaving the door open for opportunity to enter. Just keep working and have confidence in yourself and your vision. It is that confidence that will inspire others to embrace and share your ideas, as well.

Don't Be Discouraged

- What if I don't make it?

- What if I fail?

- What if people don't like me?

- What if I am scorned or mocked?

These are all the negative voices that pop into your head time and time again. It is human nature to doubt oneself sometimes, especially during times of extreme adversity or uncertainty. It is so easy to get discouraged when things do not go your way. You simply have to understand that these voices are not you. They have no value and no ability to hurt you, unless you begin to listen to them and believe what they are saying. Simply refuse to pay them any mind. Stay focused on your success path and do not allow any external or internal voices dissuade you from attaining your goals.

If you do not believe in you, then no one else will. You have to fight and continue fighting for what you want, despite your own inner doubts and insecurities. Learn to use these voices to inspire you to work harder and grow a tougher skin against all naysayers, including the voices inside your own head.

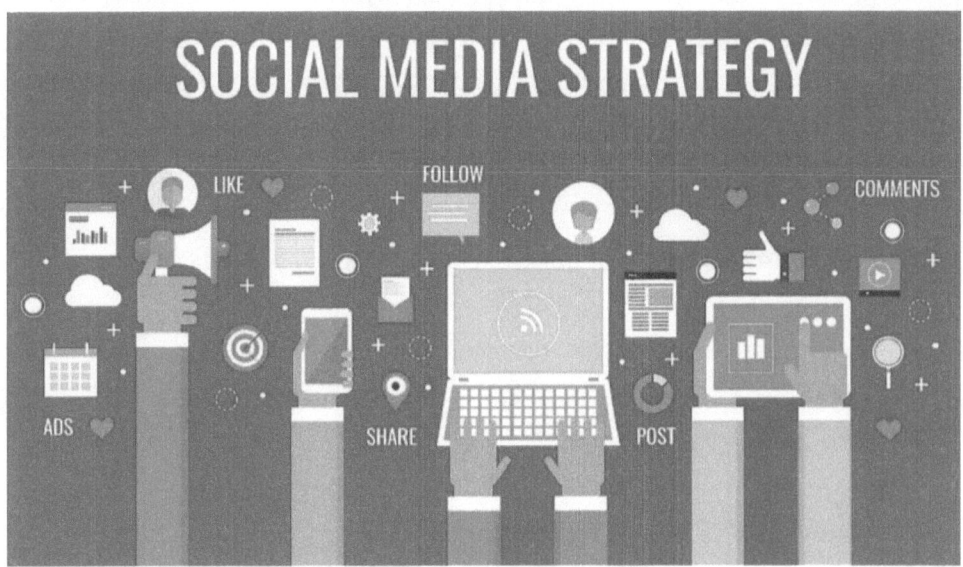

Part 4:
Business Lessons 101

What are Social Metrics?

Social metrics (also called social media metrics) are a very important concept for influencers to understand. Social media metrics are measurable statistics that can be attributed to a particular causation. As an influencer, you often want your followers to perform a specific action. You use your influence to persuade people to perform this action and the results of this effort can be measured in terms of success. This is a metric. To put it simply, social metrics allow the tracking of influencer campaigns to see how well they perform.

You should be tracking your own social metrics as much as possible. It is 100% sure that any company which partners with you will track your metrics closely. You want to continuously improve your social metrics by trying varying strategies and then using a combination of the best tactics to form a very persuasive approach that optimizes the effectiveness of interactions with your audience going forward.

Some of the important social metrics to keep your eye on include:

- How many people see a post.

- How many people interact with a post.

- How many people share a post.

- How many people actually perform a specific desired action.

All of these metrics are valuable statistics unto themselves, but how they interact together will really determine how effective you are as a social influencer. Let's look at the following examples:

- Having a huge reach is great (lots of people seeing a post).

- Getting lots of likes on that post is slightly more important.

- Receiving relevant comments on that post is exponentially more important. However, receiving irrelevant comments undermines the success of the post.

- Getting lots of shares is always great, but who is sharing the post and with whom? One share from a real influencer is worth 10,000 or more shares by normal readers with virtually no influential reach.

- Having followers actually perform the action that you are trying to get them to do is the best measure of success during a campaign. It is more important than all of the above metrics put together. If your user clicks, buys, signs up or does whatever it is they should do in an optimal scenario, then you have succeeded in reaching your post objective with that user 100%.

Therefore, although having an army of followers who see and like posts every day is great, having a smaller following who sees, likes and ACTS on your post will make you a much more powerful and paid influencer. This is an extremely vital concept to understand. Being successful as an influencer is MUCH MORE complicated than simply having lots of followers...

Collaborations and Making Money

Collaborations are a great way to increase your influence and make awesome creative connections on any social platform. Collaboration can be a partnership between 2 or more content creators working together or can be a business arrangement between an influencer and a sponsor business. Both of these possibilities are what you are trying to accomplish as an influencer in any niche!

Creative collaborations can be as simple as going to a place or event together, helping each other take photos, produce video, write an account, work together on a project or do whatever it is that you do. Visual creators certainly benefit from having collaborators, especially if they do not have a dedicated person to follow them and document all their activities every day. A collaborator provides a unique perspective to posts and will also lend their creativity to whatever it is you are doing together.

When you collaborate with another creator, you should always credit them for whatever they did to help you. Be sure to tag them in any post they worked on, so that the content will show up in their feed, as well. This tagging will provide them with content, announce your collaboration and also expose their audience to your work, as well. It is a win/win situation all around!

It is no wonder that many influencers are continuously collaborating on many projects with many people at once. Collaboration harnesses the power of multiple creators and multiple audiences to boost a post's popularity to heights never thought possible in some cases!

Your collaborators will also often become your friends and allies. These are people working in the same or similar niches to you and it is in both of your interests to partner up and grow your brands in synergy with one another whenever possible. You can be much more productive together and can even benefit from less financial investment than it would cost each of you individually when you share posts, work together, split expenses and both actively promote the post to your established and new followers. There are just so many benefits of collaborations for creators, the audience and the niche, in general.

The other very important type of collaboration is the variety that pays you or directly benefits your audience in some way (coupons, offers, discount codes). Companies are actively looking to work with successful influencers. They want to harness the social leverage which you have built and are willing to pay you to do it and/or reward your followers.

Partnerships with companies and sponsor organizations will form much of the financial profitability for most influencer businesses, so these collaborations are very important. If you can successfully collaborate with a sponsor long-term, you can actually make the dream of getting paid to do what you love a sustainable reality. Let's look at these financially-motivated collaborations deeper in a separate section for more clarity...

Commercial Partnerships

Companies are always looking to work with successful influencers. They know that these people speak directly to an audience of potential customers and have already built trust and authority with these people. It takes a company a tremendous amount of time and money to build a similar authority and trust arrangement.

Proven research has shown that using an influencer to market products and services is exponentially more effective than other forms of cold advertising and even many types of targeted advertising. Among young people in particular, influencer reviews and endorsements have much more credibility than any other type of company advertising and have proven themselves to be a great investment for commercial entities to make.

Let's look at some obvious income streams that can come from collaborating with a sponsor company:

- You can share their content with your followers on a per post basis or as an ongoing contract. Of course, you can announce that you are affiliated together, which lends your face, voice and creativity to the company 24/7.

- You can get paid to create and promote company products or services to your followers. Typically, the ad will be very organic, integrating you and the product or service naturally together to make it much less like an ad and much more like a valuable personal recommendation to your fans.

- You can act as a brand ambassador, lending your name, face and social presence to work for a company doing many promotional activities. The company might even help you to grow during this process by exposing you to a new audience on different types of media. Many influencers take such opportunities to transition into different media outlets, like television or film.

- You might receive discount or free products and/or services, or monetary compensation, for any of these possible arrangements. Your audience might also be rewarded in terms of discounts, offers or other special considerations. These deals are beneficial to you also, since followers will really appreciate a good offer that materializes because of you...

Be Professional!

If you want your business to grow and become a respected brand, you MUST be professional. This is especially true when dealing with sponsors and collaborators. If you can not present yourself professionally, you will never be taken seriously and therefore, your brand will hit a glass ceiling in terms of growth potential in short order.

Not everyone has the benefit of a university business degree or experience dealing in the manner in which proper business is conducted. However, everyone can learn or hire professional representation!

There are tons of resources available online for free that can help you to learn how to speak to corporations and how to best represent yourself, your passion and your value proposition in a clear and professional way. Here are some important considerations when it comes to being professional:

- Learn how to communicate using business language.

- Do not use slang, profanity or unclear language when dealing with companies or business partners of any kind.

- Make sure your website looks stellar and really represents who you are!

- Get business cards made up! Carry them and use them in the real world to promote yourself and your brand. This small addition to a marketing strategy can go a long way when it comes to presenting your best foot forward!

- Do not undervalue yourself. Do not overvalue yourself. When discussing terms of commercial agreements, offer your services at a fair rate commensurate with your actual value proposition. Accurate valuation will make you much more professional and will help create a sustainable and predictable income for you moving forward.

- If you grow large enough to warrant the expense, consider hiring a manager, agent and/or lawyer to help you to perform your business dealings correctly. Although these services are expensive, they will also usually cause you to earn more and be taken much more seriously by large sponsors.

Do I REALLY Want to Be Sponsored?

Let's talk about the pros and cons of collaborating with company sponsors. First, let's examine the benefits:

- You make money.

- You get free stuff or discounted stuff.

- You might gain additional exposure on different forms of media.

- You will raise your position among your peers by working with large, reputable companies.

- You will raise your value for future collaborations by working with reputable companies, especially over time.

- Your followers might get direct benefits, as well, which they will surely appreciate!

Ok, so what are the downsides of sponsorship?

- Your followers might not appreciate being marketed to, especially constantly. Your credibility could suffer dramatically.

- Some posts become more like obvious ads than social shares. Blatant advertising usually performs poorly compared to more focused unsponsored content sharing.

- Backlash can result, including loss of followers, negative comments or loss of creative collaborators in some instances.

- You might not know everything about a company and eventually discover that you disagree with certain things about their business model, history or practices.

- Any of these negative consequences could potentially ruin all of your hard work, effectively ending your business forever.

Many companies are predatory on social media. There are countless companies that actively recruit new up-and-coming influencers to sell for them. These companies will present a slick proposal stating that they will give you a discount code for you followers and provide you with some small benefit, such as a free item or additional personal discount in exchange for some sponsored post or ambassadorship.

Since many aspiring influencers are desperate to see some return for all their work, they take these companies up on these one-sided offers that make the company lots of sales, but usually lead to the influencer losing status and making no real gains financially.

I strongly recommend avoiding any such collaboration until you are well established and can dictate the terms that suit you and fairly compensate you for your work and results. Don't sell your soul and post tons of sponsored content just to get a free stupid bracelet or bathing suit... It is just not worth it at all! I tend to tell companies that they have the chance to hire me now at a good price, because I am growing every day and tomorrow I will be more expensive, and more, and more...

A good general rule is to let your lawyer or manager handle your business affairs whenever possible. If you are not big enough to have a business lawyer or manager, then you probably should not be considering paid collaborations yet! You will likely get the crap end of the deal.

Go Find Sponsors

If you decide that you do want sponsors, do not sit passively for them to come to you! Instead, go out and get them, just like you have already done when trying to increase your follower base. Be proactive and contact individuals and companies that are a good fit for your brand image and niche. However, before leaping into action, be sure that you are ready to engage these people and companies professionally:

- Create a business proposition letter that can be easily tailored to specific needs. In this letter, tell the potential sponsor what you can offer and what you expect in return. You can use this letter to receive free products and services that can be enjoyed yourself or passed along to your followers in the form of a giveaway.

- Make sure to have a section on your website where potential sponsors can contact you easily. Be sure to check this contact method daily for any new responses. Similarly, be certain to have contact information easily accessible on all of your social media platforms so that people and companies who are interested in working with you can get in touch without any hassle.

- When talking with prospective sponsors, be confident about what you can do for them. Have statistics and social metrics ready to back up your claims. Never over-promise and under-deliver. Instead, over-deliver on every campaign and your brand's value will soar!

- Be flexible as to what type of compensation you will accept for social campaigns. Sure, money is always desirable, but accepting products or services from the person or company is likely to give you more value, since this compensation costs them less than actual cash.

- Always seek to work long-term with sponsors that are good fits. Before any social campaign ends, re-contact the sponsor with your ideas for the next step in working together. Try to maintain relationships long-term and periodically re-contact former sponsors for new gigs as is reasonable.

How Else Can I Make Money?

Besides collaborations, there are many ways for you to benefit financially from your influencer status. Let's explore some of the best and most common routes to economic gain:

It is easy to receive perks from many businesses that you do not work with during formal collaborations. In some cases, your reputation will precede you and these businesses might offer you free products or services in exchange for a mention on your social media.

In other cases, you might have to provide an offer to mention a business in exchange for some benefit. The possibilities here are endless. You can receive free or discounted travel, consumer products, accommodations, healthcare services, beauty services, consultations and virtually anything else that has financial value!

Some influencers rarely pay for anything at all and in fact, tend to accumulate tons of free stuff that is sent to them on the chance that they might mention it in a post... As a travel influencer, I routinely benefit when it comes to the cost of transportation, accommodations and activities, but also get additional benefits in terms of booking priority, no-hassle cancelation and the virtual guarantee that I will have a great experience wherever I may go!

There are many ways to monetize your website and social feed, including the use of ad networks, affiliate arrangements and through the sale of your own products or services. If you are adept at monetization of web properties, you will soon realize how many options you truly have and how much potential passive income is possible! Therefore, it is good to become educated on this topic if you do not have this knowledge already.

Speaking of your services, if you offer public services of any kind, promoting yourself through your social influencer posts is a great way to get tons of gigs. Musicians, artists and all manner of service providers can promote themselves and their work to an audience of people who actually want to patronize you. This is a huge benefit of influencer reach and success!

You can use the skills you have built during your social influencer business development to help others who need assistance with their influencer businesses or web projects, such as website building, social media management, content creation and consultancy.

You can use your notoriety to springboard yourself into other industries and potentially develop an even bigger and more lucrative career in some related field. Literature, television and film are all within reach for a successful influencer.

There are countless ways that you can make money once you have a focused audience that listens to you. It was one of the first rules of the modern internet and remains very true today: TRAFFIC is KING. If you have the numbers, making money from your traffic is simple. If you do not have the numbers, then making substantial money will always be difficult. Therefore, the goal is to continue to grow your social presence until your following is truly vast and wide-ranging. This audience will provide all the opportunities you will ever need to literally get rich from your influencer business.

The most difficult part is getting some money to start coming in. Once you open your doors to monetization potential through a large following of loyal and engaged supporters, then the money valve will literally open wide and will not stop unless you do something wrong... You will probably have to work diligently for some time before making even one dollar from your new business. However, it is certainly possible to realize very large financial gains in a short time period once you become established, trusted and in-demand. Just be sure to keep all the strategies in mind which have been previously discussed, in order to help you to return value to the very followers who have made you successful!

Merchandise

Merchandise, now commonly known in the influencer industry as merch, is a great way to make money and promote your brand. What could be better than a person paying you to wear an item of clothing or use a product that bears your name? Seriously!

Merchandise is a great way to earn and reach more potential followers in the real world, courtesy of the person who bought and uses the product. However, it can also be a way to lose money and annoy your followers, so utilizing a merchandise strategy should be well planned, with each step considered carefully.

If you sell merchandise, you will hopefully make money on each item you sell. There are so many options when it comes to making and shipping these items, so be certain to do your research on the best model to fit your specific needs.

Generally, the more quantity of an item you can purchase at once, and the more you can do yourself in terms of the logistics of packing and shipping, then the more money you will make. The more you rely on single orders being made-to-order and drop-shipped by the company that makes the product, the less money you will make. However, the tradeoff here is time...

When making more money, the time commitment will be much greater, as will your financial investment upfront. When using made-to-order and drop-ship services, you will need to invest nothing more than time to create the products and then all the rest of the process is automated for you.

Of course, if you grow large enough, you can hire dedicated staff or a subcontractor company to handle merchandise creation and fulfillment on your behalf. If you reach this stage, you will know what to do already, since you have proven yourself a very capable influencer to attain such success!

Be cautious about merchandising when there is no demand. If lots of people are asking you for merchandise regularly, then you MUST start selling it. However, if your audience is small to medium and no one is asking, then pestering these few supporters to buy your crap will probably only push them away.

Never over-merchandise to your followers, no matter how large and successful you become. It becomes a major liability when people begin to see you as a money-making entity, more than a valuable part of their social media life.

Plan on Working Harder Than Ever!

Don't make the mistake that so many small to medium influencers make! Once some measure of success comes their way, they stop working hard and start enjoying the fruits of their labor too much! This is why so few of these people ever make it to the upper echelon of influencer success. Once you start to gain momentum, it is time to work harder than ever to firmly establish yourself at the very top of your niche as a true superstar of social influence.

If you can push harder, do more, achieve more and influence more, then you will continue to grow. Don't try to monetize every opportunity when you are still small or medium in your following size. The amount of benefit gained will not be enough to justify the downsides of using your influence to profit at this stage of the game.

If you can make money without jeopardizing your growth, then that is great. However, do not focus on money too early in your business or else you will create your own glass ceiling that will be difficult to break through. Instead, work harder than ever before to grow until you have little, if any, competition in you niche. At this stage, the money will come much easier anyway and will be much more than you could have earned previously.

The lesson here is not to get caught up making pennies when you can be making real money later on. Strive towards the top of the mountain first and allow the money to come to you once you arrive. This is a great rule for many things in life and it certainly applies to virtually all online businesses, including being a social influencer.

Don't get lazy. Get don't complacent. If you have not achieved much success, don't lose hope. Just continually re-strategize to make sure that you are doing everything correctly and keep working. Those who persevere will reap the rewards. Those who quit can not and will not ever taste victory. It really is that simple...

How Big Does My Influence Need to Be?

Many up-and-coming influencers ask me, "How big does my following need to be? How much influence must I have in order to be successful?"

My answer is... How big can you make it? More followers with a deeper level of trust and engagement will always benefit you tangibly.

If you can keep building, then do so until you decide that it is time to move on to something else. If you do make this decision, then enjoy the money that will keep coming for a short time afterwards, but realize that the well of financial benefits will dry up very quickly in the age of short-lived social influence.

You can always take time for breaks when you feel overworked and exhausted. In fact, if you have built your business correctly to a successful degree already, then you can use your rest time to continue to grow your follower base thorough targeted posts that will allow you to explore new avenues of both creativity and collaboration.

Look for a healthy cycle of pushing and then maintaining in your influencer business. You can not hustle 24/7 indefinitely. You will burn out. Take time to level-off a bit every once in a while, taking short breaks when you can. Use your social posts to announce planned breaks by traveling or partnering with hospitality providers to get some much needed R&R for free and use the opportunity to fuel your creativity when you post again.

The population of the world is increasing dramatically day by day. If you are not growing, then you are actually shrinking in your influence. No matter how successful you are, you can always become more successful in the future, exploiting new opportunities and making new fans. I always suggest making the continual growth of your business as a top priority, since this objective will serve you better than any other, as long as you go about accomplishing it ethically and responsibly.

Reinvest in Your Brand

It is vital to reinvest in your brand as you grow! If you start living off all the money you earn, it is likely that the money will soon level off and begin to diminish over time. If you really want to succeed long-term, and to a substantial degree, then it is really important to reinvest in your business. This includes committing resources of time, effort and money!

I recommend reinvesting all the money you can, up to 100% whenever possible, for as long as possible. You will see tangible rewards for each dollar reinvested wisely. Wisely is indeed the key word here...

Here are some examples of quality reinvestments of time and money that will help you to reach new levels of success:

- Spend on experiences that can be documented and shared on your social media channels. These can include travel, events, purchases, giveaways or anything that is relevant to your niche. The more you have to share, the more your audience will appreciate your work and your business will grow. If you consistently share the same things over and over, you will not grow, so reinvest in experiences that will translate into better, more diverse and more engaging posts.

- Advertising can really help to catapult you to the next level of social stardom. Sponsored posts are guaranteed to get your work in front of many new eyes and as long as you track the performance of these posts and engage your new audience actively, you can convert many of these people into followers in no time at all.

- Hire subcontractors to make your work look better. There are tons of excellent support staff who can help to make your posts perform optimally, as well as support staff who can help you to manage particular aspects of your business that are time-consuming and low return on time invested. It is often best to contract these tasks out so that you have the time and energy to devote to the things you do best... creating content and engaging directly with your audience.

There are also things that you can spend time and money on that are never good investments and some of these things can actually ruin your business and destroy all of the hard work you already invested in your social network:

- Cheating is never a good way to achieve any goal. Buying followers is strictly a NO NO and does not fool anyone. You might have 100,000 followers, but if you do not get the right number and type of regular engagement, everyone will know FOR SURE that you are a fraud. Furthermore, it is against the terms of service of many social networks to engage in deceptive practices, such as purchasing fake followers. If discovered, and you will be eventually, you will be banned and your business will be gone. Don't do it!

- Often investing in a package where a company claims to "do everything" for you at a low cost so that you will grow quickly and succeed "overnight" is a great waste of money. These companies use deceptive practices like bots and software hacks to provide seeming benefits that are actually detrimental to your profile, posts and business. Do not support these scammers, thieves, liars, miscreants and general a--holes. Invest in top quality sub-contractors at fair market value or do the work yourself!

- Investing in advertising, but not following up with the actual people who see your posts, is rarely successful or cost effective. Paying for a sponsored post and then ignoring all the people who see it is a huge waste of time and money. Make sure to capitalize on every dollar spent by setting aside time to engage new audience members actively and converting them to followers.

Giveaways

Giveaways are such a great way to reinvest in your business. Some of my favorite influencers reinvest a significant part of their income into giveaways for their audience and sacrifice their own short-term financial success to further their big picture objectives.

The idea of giveaways is to directly reward your audience for following and supporting you by literally giving them stuff. There are so many things you can offer on your own or by partnering with companies who can absorb some or all of the promotional cost:

- Literal giveaways of products or services are a great way to get people interested in you. Everyone loves free stuff, especially if the item is high value and featured often on your network. You can give away items you review, items specifically acquired for contests and prizes offered by sponsors. The more stuff you can give away, the better.

Remember that people who follow you just for your giveaways are not really loyal, so you will either have to keep giving stuff away continuously or win them over to become followers while you have their limited window of attention. I recommend doing both whenever possible!

- Discounts, coupons and special offers are always appreciated if they add real value to a transaction that a follower might want anyway. Low value discounts, or discounts on undesirable products or services, will not succeed and might even create a backlash effect of causing you to lose followers, so choose your partnership offers wisely and carefully.

- Use your giveaways to increase engagement and add to your social metrics. Require people to enter the chance to win a giveaway by participating openly in some action. Make them leave a comment, take a poll or otherwise perform some interaction that will increase your engagement for a post or campaign.

- If you consistently give away great stuff, you can build a really awesome engagement metric from the contests alone and can even put your followers to work for you by creating much of the content that you actually share! This is a win-win for all involved and can lead to a fast-track to social success!

- Remember that giveaways often involve special considerations and should be open to everybody. This might require the ability to ship items worldwide in some cases, so be sure to do your due diligence as to the logistics of giving away stuff BEFORE you promise to do it!

Be Generous

Generosity is one of the most endearing of all personality traits. Generosity can also be incredibly beneficial to your influencer career path! I suggest learning the value of being generous early on and increasing your level of "giving back" as your move forward in your professional growth.

Why should you be generous? Primarily, you should give back since it is just the right thing to do in life. If you live just for yourself, then you will soon find yourself alone. It's really that simple. People value generosity and can be especially critical of anyone who is successful, but does not give back enough...

How can you be generous? Let's explore some easy examples of how you can be giving in your new career path:

- Mentoring up-and-coming influencers and creators in your niche is a great way to show generosity and gain loyalty and respect from the people who receive it, as well as from the people who objectively observe it.

- Don't nickel and dime your business partners. In fact, be generous to them. If they help to support you, offer them more than they are paying for on a consistent basis. Providing great value will give you a fantastic reputation and will lead to better sponsor retention, as well as new sponsorship opportunities.

- Always give back to your followers. We discussed giveaways already and actually giving them something is a great idea. However, don't neglect to give them your ear and your heart. Listen to them, engage them and interact with them.

They are the reason you are successful. Make sure to thank them regularly and sincerely with thoughts, words and actions.

- Get involved in quality good causes. Donate your time and resources to help causes that are worthy. Getting involved in good works will help you to grow in ways you can not imagine and give you access to great networking and sponsorship opportunities.

Avoid the Slippery Slope!

The slipperiest slope in social media is certainly success! Once you become successful and are ahead of your competition, this is your truest test. Remember, the best always have targets on their backs.

Your up-and-coming competitors will see you and track everything you do all of the time. Meanwhile, since you are ahead of them, they are in your rearview mirror and what they are doing will largely be invisible to you. Therefore, you must know that they are on your heels and work hard to remain ahead in this competitive race to the top of the success mountain:

- Don't take unnecessary breaks from work.

- Don't ignore or underestimate your competition.

- Don't make enemies.

- Don't compromise your brand image or personal values.

- Don't fall into a rut and lose your creativity.

- Don't think that what you are doing to achieve success today will continue to work tomorrow. This is a fast moving industry and best practices are in constant evolution. If you stop growing, you will immediately begin shrinking in social influence. This is an absolute rule. Do whatever you can to stay ahead of the curve and diversify your approach to social success each and every day. Better yet, create the trends as a true influencer and then you will always be ahead of the curve!

Social influencers come and go. Some seem so hugely successful and influential that their brands look indestructible. However, this is just an illusion. No one is immune to time, over-exposure, ego or mistakes. Therefore, it is best to plan that your success might not endure forever, but do everything you can day to day to ensure that it will!

Become a Household Name

If you follow the guidelines set forth in this book and work harder than you ever imagined possible, you might just reach the pinnacle of your niche. At this stage, enjoy your success!

People know you. People love you. Most importantly, people are willing to pay you to work with them on many different projects. You have taken your social influence to the top! What is the next step?

You have proven that you can do whatever you put your mind to. There is really nothing stopping you. Remember that a career as a social influencer might not last forever. Use your opportunity to create new avenues of success for yourself and do everything you can to build a sustainable business model that will transcend the passing trends and fashions of the time.

In order to attain this level of success, you have acquired so many marketable skills. Use them and challenge yourself to do whatever your heart desires.

Make sure to invest your earnings wisely to make your success really endure even once your social fame diminishes. If you do things correctly, you will never have to work every again and will be able to pursue whatever it is you DO want to do from this day forward.

You have achieved the dream that so many people quest for. You work for yourself, doing something you love on your own terms. You have reached to pinnacle of your profession and now have chances to do much more with your life. Make these opportunities count!

Most importantly, be sure to give back and help others to achieve similar successes. In the end, our legacy lives on not in ourselves, but in the things we can do to help others grow beyond us. This is the way to really mark your life a true success.

Get Help - Consult with Me

Do you need help with your influencer business now or at any time in the future? If so, I can help you! I am available to assist you in growing your business and can custom tailor my consultation to match your needs. Only have a couple of quick questions? That's fine! It will not cost you much to get my ear and allow my voice to guide you. Need more help or ongoing help? I can do that also... Reach out and let's discuss what you need. I love mentoring people who are following their dreams! I can be contacted anytime at my email: jammyjourney@gmail.com

About Me

The first thing you should know is that "me" is actually "us"! Jammy Journey is a couple (Jammy and Adam) who has worked together fulltime online since 2006. Our extraordinary lifestyle has come about from our own hard work and all of our money has been earned using the internet business model ethically and responsibly.

We have created many websites since 2006. We have written and published over 15 books. We have also created a range of influencer brands spanning many different niches. We have extensive experience in virtually all aspects of online businesses. We are not household names, since most of our work has been in very specific and non-mainstream niches, such as helping people with various health and lifestyle issues.

Our business model has bought us the one thing we all truly want: Freedom. We can travel as we see fit, live anywhere in the world and continue to earn as we pursue doing the things we love to do! We have taken the opportunity to do good things for our world and the sentient life which lives upon it!

We are very active in planetary activism, with particular focuses on preserving the oceans and stopping plastic pollution on our beautiful Earth. We are nature lovers and use our voices to help protect our Mother Earth against all manner of threats. We fight for animal rights and against all manner of abuses to intelligent life on our planet. Most of all, we encourage activism in others, helping people to understand that you do not need to be a radical! Every little bit of positive energy counts. We encourage you to be part of the solution, rather than just another part of the problem. Being knowledgeable and active in planetary issues is indeed cool!

At this stage of our lives, we choose our projects based on their desirability to our souls, rather than profitability. We have made money and continue to do so. Therefore, we are free to do the things we really enjoy all the time. We love martial arts, music, photography and making films. Since we have many projects going at once, we do not need to invest ourselves into any one to the point of being stressed. This makes life a great adventure and provides us plenty of time to live in the now! We highly recommend learning more about presence and how a simple paradigm shift in attention will open doors for you that you never imagined possible!

Copyright and Legal Notice

www.ingramcontent.com/pod-product-compliance
Lightning Source LLC
Chambersburg PA
CBHW030719220526
45463CB00005B/2112